THE TRAIN ROBBING BUNCH

Rick Miller

THE EARLY WEST SERIES
CREATIVE PUBLISHING COMPANY
BOX 9292, PH 713 846 7907
COLLEGE STATION, TEXAS 77840

Miller, Rick, 1941—
 The train robbing Bunch.

  (The Early West series)
  Bibliography: p.
  Includes index.
   1. Bunch, Eugene Franklin, 1843-1894. 2. Train robberies—Southwest, Old—History—19th century. 3. Southwest, Old—History. 4. Outlaws—Southwest, Old—Biography. 5. Southwest, Old—Biography. I. Title. II. Series.
F396.B9M54   1983   976'.041   82-22204

ISBN 0-932702—25—2 (hardback)
ISBN 0—932702—27—9 (softback)
ISBN 0—932702—26—0 (collector's edition)

Collector's leatherbound edition, 25 copies
Regular hardback edition, 1500 copies
Softback edition, 1500 copies

First Edition, First Printing

Copyrighted by Creative Publishing Company, 1983, Early West Series, Box 9292, Ph. 713-846-7907, College Station, Texas 77840

Dedicated to

Mom and Shelli

4   The Train Robbing Bunch

Table of Contents

	Introduction	7
1	The Early Years	11
2	The Civil War	26
3	Gone to Texas	37
4	Outlaw Beginnings	55
5	Robbery in Louisiana	75
6	Escape West	100
7	In Pursuit of Bunch	114
8	The End of Bunch	128
9	Aftermath	141
	Bibliography	160
	Index	168
	The Author, Rick Miller	174

Introduction

Research into the careers of the colorful personalities who figured prominently in the history of the Old East has traditionally focused on the more famous or infamous: Wild Bill Hickok, Billy the Kid, Wyatt Earp, Jesse James, and many others all too familiar, even to those without any expertise in the genre. Because these men received widespread notoriety while still alive, and in many cases shamelessly exploited that attention, they ultimately became larger than life. The legends built around their deeds achieved heroic proportions, capturing the public fancy and assuring them a permanent place in American folklore. Books, motion pictures, and television episodes have retold the exploits of these characters with highly varying degrees of inaccuracy, continuing to perpetuate them as important figures in the development of the western frontier.

Only in recent years has there been a new focus on other men and women of the time; lesser known figures just as colorful, but who, for some reason, did not achieve or sustain the fame of the others. Eugene Bunch was one of these. "Captain Bunch" achieved brief notoriety that passed quickly. One of the last train robbers (as well as the first known to rob a train single-handedly) in a time when American society was leaving the frontier behind, Bunch became lost to history, at best only a footnote in the lore of American banditry.

There is now beginning to be more of an emphasis on a scholarly, objective approach to the personalities and events of the Nineteenth Century. Too much of what has passed for historical research in this area has been shamelessly sloppy. The trend seems to be reversing, however, and historians are taking greater pains to set the record straight through careful, accurate, factual documentation from which logical conclusions can be drawn and defended. This book is meant to be a contribution to that effort.

Eugene Bunch first came to my attention during the course of research into the early history of law enforcement in Texas' Dallas County. While the likes of the Younger Brothers, Belle Starr, Sam Bass, Doc Holliday, Luke Short, Mysterious Dave Mather, and others crossed Dallas' dusty streets, there were lesser known contemporaries, such as Bunch, who were also a part of the scene. As I subsequently became more involved in learning about the outlaws and lawmen of the Old West, the enigma of Bunch intrigued me. As with his more notorious peers, he perpetrated bold and daring deeds; he was marked by a unique, dynamic individuality; and, as with so many others, he died violently, a hunted man. Yet, unlike the others, Bunch came to outlawry later in life. He had received an adequate education and achieved a reasonably successful career as a teacher, county clerk, real estate agent, and newspaper editor. What would drive a man such as this to change his life's direction, after he was forty years old, to pursue the risky path that Bunch chose? Most outlaws had played out their string well before the age of thirty.

Bunch was basically a loner. There might even be an argument that he ultimately sealed his own doom by involving others in his last major robbery, deviating from his normal method of operation. Those critical character flaws which led him to the outlaw trail, and which he was apparently unable to control, ultimately demeaned him as an individual and one comes away with an impression of an amoral man. There seems to be no indication of any regret on his part for the things he did: abandonment of family, forgery, adultery, robbery, and murder. Yet, he was an intelligent, good-humored man and well-liked by his personal contemporaries. The answer, unfortunately, can only be surmised.

In telling the story of Eugene Bunch, I have attempted to let the facts speak for themselves where possible. In many areas there is adequate documentation that leads to fairly obvious conclusions. In other areas, however, the story is often dependent on sketchy and conflicting newspaper accounts, always subject to unreliable reporting and exaggeration. Where there are significant disputes as to certain events, I have included the different versions and leave it to the reader to come to his own conclusions, if possible. The approach is chronological, almost tediously so at certain points, in order to trace Bunch's progression into outlawry and to provide the most definitive account of his life. Where I take the liberty of editorializing or reaching some conclusion, especially in the absence of documentation, it is generally done on the basis of a personal feel for Bunch's overall life and the times in which he lived. Of course, where there are incorrect conclusions or inaccuracies, the responsibility is mine.

The reader will also note that there are some loose ends here and there in the telling of the story that might deserve further exploration. Again, I accept responsibility. While the intention of this book was to be as complete and accurate as possible, no history is ever really complete nor research finished. Hopefully, additional research in the future will help fill the gaps.

No such effort can be complete without acknowledging those persons who helped make it possible. First and foremost, I owe a real debt of gratitude to a stately Southern lady, Mrs. Zuma Fendlason Magee of Franklinton, Louisiana. She was the first to recognize the uniqueness of Bunch's life and in 1975, in her eighty-third year, compiled a manuscript of newspaper articles and other materials dealing with him. We developed a lively correspondence and she has shared my enthusiasm for this project, contributing much to its completion. It was her husband's uncle who was murdered by Bunch in 1892, when she was seven months old. In her own right, she is an accomplished and nationally respected genealogist and takes great pride in her involvement with the annual Washington Parish Fair, an outstanding example of a local effort to preserve the past. Mrs. Magee's zest for living and growing has indeed been an inspiration. I am also indebted to Daunton Gibbs of Franklinton; Mrs. Vickie Knight and her son, Hunter, of Franklinton; and Mrs. Irma Lampton of Tylertown, Mississippi, who, along with Mrs. Magee, turned a steamy Louisiana Saturday into a day of exciting discovery about Captain Bunch and Curnell Hobgood. A special debt of thanks also goes to Patricia Sanders and her brother, Ricky Scott, for guiding us to the site of Bunch's death.

In addition, I am truly appreciative for the gracious assistance of Curnell Hobgood's remaining son, Tom Hobgood, West Monroe, Louisiana, who, at a lively seventy-six years of age, patiently fielded my questions and recalled his father to help set the record straight. In addition, Mr. Jim Erwin, 91, son-in-law of the Curnell, Bogalusa, Louisiana, provided invaluable input.

Mrs. Rastus Hobgood, South Walthall County, Mississippi, was extremely helpful in locating the Curnell's grave as well as sharing the family history. Mrs. Audrey Johnson, South Walthall County, Mississippi, graciously shared a photograph of her grandfather, the "Curnell," and also provided important information. I am indebted to Mrs. Leroy James of Covington, Louisiana, for assistance in getting a copy of the photograph.

Valuable assistance was also provided by Linda Touraine and Joella Orr of the Denton, Texas, Public Library; Lucille Boykin, Dallas Public Library; Frank Scoggins, Cooke County, Texas, Clerk; Warren Flowers, editor, *Gainesville* (Texas) *Daily Register*; E. Q. Richards, Mississippi Genealogical Association, Macon, Mississippi; Stephen M. Findlay, Memphis/Shelby County, Tennessee, Public Library and Information Center; James D. Horan, Little Falls, New Jersey; Charlene C. Cain, Archives and Records Service, Louisiana Secretary of State's Office; Ann Malone, United Daughters of the Confederacy, Richmond, Virginia; Marie M. Fogg, Deputy Court Clerk, East Feliciana Parish,

Louisiana; Mrs. Pat Leeper, Louisiana State Library; Don P. Morrison, Photo-duplication Library, Louisiana State Library; Marjorie Crowson, Tangipahoa Parish, Louisiana, Library; Deborah L. Rothman, Illinois Central Gulf Railroad; George F. O'Neill, Pinkerton's Inc.; Collin B. Hamer, Jr., and Wayne E. Everard, New Orleans, Louisiana, Public Library; Carol M. Finney, Texas State Archives, Austin; and Irene Morris, Camp Moore Museum, Tangipahoa, Louisiana.

Also appreciated was the assistance of the Kemp Public Library, Wichita Falls, Texas; The National Archives and Records Service, Washington, D.C.; the Texas Department of Health, Austin; the *Wichita Falls* (Texas) *Times and Record News*; the North Texas State University Library, Denton, Texas; the Baylor University Texas Collection, Waco, Texas; Mrs. Dixie Moss, Baton Rouge, Louisiana; Mrs. Marilyn Bunch Hart, Kentwood, Louisiana; Barbara Gibson, Assistant Clerk, City of Delhi, Louisiana; Chuck Branton, Richland Parish Library, Louisiana; the Mississippi Department of Archives and History, Jackson, Mississippi; and Jo Green, Tyler, Texas, Public Library.

A special debt of thanks is owed my sister, Mrs. Karen Cartier, for interpreting my numerous scribbles and annotations and typing the manuscript in a presentable form.

Rick Miller
Waco, Texas
April 20, 1982

1 The Early Years

Occasionally on a quiet summer evening, in the lingering heat of a disappearing Texas sun, the story of "Eugene Bundy"[1] is recalled by oldtimers for their young listeners. They tell how "Bundy", though respected by the citizens of Gainesville and elected the Cooke County Clerk, maintained a cool distance from others. His jealous wife daily rode her bay horse, Queen Anne, to the courthouse and then rode home with him, ever mindful of rumors of his dalliances with both a local school teacher and a "questionable woman" known as Belle. Numerous relatives had come to live with the Bundys, crowding his house and expecting him to support them.

The legend describes a series of stagecoach holdups by a lone highwayman in the "Black Hollow," a wooded dell of oak trees six miles west of town. The mails were regularly rifled, but the local sheriff was hesitant to pursue the desperado. The mysterious, tall "Eugene Bundy" and his horse, Black Prince, were strangely absent from town each time a robbery occurred. One day, the "Bundy family" disappeared forever from Cooke County and, so the story goes, the scarlet Belle led the sheriff to a heap of empty mail bags and a taunting note from "Bundy" admitting the crimes.

As with other legends and tales passed down from generation to generation, the story of "Eugene Bundy" has been told and retold, each new version shaped to fit a more fanciful picture of what actually happened those many years ago. And also with each retelling, "Eugene Bundy" assumed a minor place among the other romantic characters who the oldtimers say roamed this North Texas area: the James boys, the Younger brothers, and Sam Bass. And perhaps, as with many other legends, there may even be a grain of truth.

In June of 1836, a twenty-one-year old Tennessee native, James Bunch, leased a section of land in the Noxubee County township of Macon in eastern Mississippi for $3,368,[2] beginning his life as a farmer. Two years later, on July 17, he married nineteen-year old Martha R. McDonald,[3] the daughter of a wealthy Mississippi planter. According to Noxubee County deed records, her father, Hugh McDonald, a generous Scot, made a gift of a number of slaves to James and Martha in April, 1840.[4] The prosperity of the Bunch family was further reflected in the 1840 Census of Noxubee County. The Bunch family had considerable land interests in Mississippi, some gained as a result of inheritance by Martha, and through the 1840's and 1850's, James Bunch made a number of major land transactions.[5] In 1844, Bunch had leased an additional 644 acres of land for $6,820 for twenty-one years.[6] In addition to being the parents of a daughter, Virginia, the couple also owned forty-four slaves, thirty of them old enough to labor in the fertile Mississippi fields.

After the birth of Theodosius C., who was known as T.C., Eugene Franklin Bunch[7] was James and Martha's third child, born on February 9, 1843.[8] When the 1850 Census was taken in Noxubee County, the listing for the growing Bunch family, however, showed only Martha and six children: Virginia, 12; T.C., 11; Eugene, 8: Laura, 6; and Mary Cornelia and Catherine, both two. Also staying with them was nineteen-year old Edward Crane of Georgia.[9] James Bunch was in California, apparently induced to leave his family by the promise of riches in the gold strike.[10] Both T.C. and Eugene were attending school at this time. Unfortunately, other than this skimpy accounting, there is very little record of the Bunch family and Eugene's early life in Mississippi.

Clearly, Bunch was born into a prominent, well-to-do family and all of the advantages that accrue to such a situation. In his early years, he was apparently conditioned to an environment of comfort and privilege typical of a wealthy antebellum

Southern planter. At the same time, his father seems to have possessed a restless spirit and was willing to pursue an adventurous course in order to experience new challenges, to find new wealth, or to perhaps escape a more mundane existence. It may be that heredity was a major force in the events that shaped Eugene Bunch's life, for clearly there was an element of dissatisfaction with the status quo underlying Bunch's later activities.

For some reason, perhaps the same restlessness, James Bunch decided to leave Mississippi and sold his land in March, 1858.[11] After selling 540 acres to Bird Ivey for $16,200,[12] he moved his growing family to eastern Louisiana. On December 27, 1858, he purchased 300 acres on the east side of Big Creek and resumed farming.[13] In the nearby small town of Franklinton, Eugene and some of his sisters attended school at Professor W. H. Dixon's Academy, which was conducted in a green-shuttered frame building across from the Parish Courthouse.[14] By 1860, James and Martha could boast eleven children living at home, ranging in age from two-and-a-half to nineteen years. Their eldest, Virginia, was no longer with the family.[15]

The late 1850's saw the growth of the crisis that would divide the nation and pit brother against brother in bloody war. Slavery as a political issue inflamed the passions of Northerner and Southerner alike and by 1860, when the first threats of secession were being voiced by Southern leaders, a few Southern states began raising local militias. The election of Abraham Lincoln in November intensified the national crisis and South Carolina subsequently seceded from the Union, followed by ten other states. Louisiana seceded on January 26, 1861. On February 8, the Confederate government was formalized and Jefferson Davis was named President. With the fall of Fort Sumter in South Carolina to Confederate forces on April 13, the Civil War had begun.

In Louisiana, a general call was promptly made for volunteers. On April 29, 1861, Camp Walker was established on the Metairie racetrack in New Orleans,[16] where a successful racing season had just ended. As thousands of eager volunteers poured into the area and were introduced to military drill and discipline, Camp Walker quickly demonstrated how unsuited it was for the mustering of an army. The encampment was surrounded by swamps and the combination of humidity with the New Orleans sewage that flowed through the area threatened widespread disease. Swarms of mosquitos and a thick muddy ooze hampered both officers and enlisted men as they tried to cope with the miserable conditions. In addition, potable drinking water was in short supply.[17] On May 13, at the direction of Louisiana Governor Moore, Brigadier General E. L. Tracy began transferring the troops by rail to a new camp named after the governor which was seventy-eight miles north of New Orleans in Tangipahoa Parish, approximately eight miles south of Mississippi. Among the units formed at Camp Walker and transferred to Camp Moore was the Fourth Louisiana Regiment, composed mostly of men from the parishes around Camp Moore. One of the companies within the regiment was Captain James H. Wingfield's "Beaver Creek Rifles."[18]

At Camp Moore, living conditions for the troops among the tall pines were much improved and nearby Beaver Creek and the Tangipahoa River provided fresh drinking water. Although it is possible that he joined other volunteers in New Orleans, military records reflect only that Eugene Bunch enlisted in Captain Wingfield's company at Camp Moore on May 25, 1861, the same date that all Louisiana military units formally organized at that time were officially transferred to the Confederate army. Wingfield's unit became Company G in the Fourth Regiment of the Louisiana Infantry, otherwise known as "Wingfield's Rifles." Bunch was one of ninety privates while his older brother, T. C., was a Third Corporal.[19]

Prior to May 25, Louisiana military units had been organized in state service with the understanding that they would be transferred to the Confederate army for an enlistment period of only twelve months. After the Third Regiment was transferred,

The Early Years   15

Jefferson Davis was named president of the Confederacy when it was formalized on January 26, 1861.

however, the Confederate War Department announced that future regiments would be accepted for no less than the duration of the war. Louisiana officials protested and urged that regiments already organized, such as the Fourth, be accepted on a twelve-month basis. The decision, of course, had a significant impact on the volunteers at Camp Moore. Finally, the Fourth Regiment was accepted on a twelve-month basis and the order was later rescinded.[20] Commanding the Fourth was Colonel Robert I. Barrow, with Lieutenant Colonel Henry Watkins Allen as second-in-command.[21]

Because military records on Bunch are so few, the most feasible approach to tracking his Civil War experiences is by following the activities of the Fourth Louisiana Regiment for that period of time during which Bunch was known to be a member. Bunch was a part of the same activities and events that marked the Fourth's role in the war. It is probably accurate to conclude that T. C. and Eugene, like so many other volunteer soldiers at the start of the Civil War, were naively eager to join in combat, their valiant mission to preserve Southern honor and tradition. Caught up in romantic notions of war that enticed thousands of others to Camp Moore, the two brothers were mustered into military life and looked forward to teaching the Yankees a lesson.

The Fourth Regiment was ordered to the Gulf Coast along the Mississippi Sound in June, 1861, to protect the area against possible Union invasion. With the regimental headquarters located at Bay St. Louis, detachments were stationed along the coastline.[22] Wingfield's company was one of three units encamped by the Mississippi City seashore in a thick grove of pine trees near the Barnes Hotel.[23] In July, the entire regiment moved to Ship Island, in the Gulf south of Biloxi, where it worked to finish construction of a fort that had been begun there by the United States some years before.[24] The troops labored under the hot sun constructing sandbag emplacements. One company mutinied and refused to work but after a confrontation with a superior number of muskets, the work stoppage was quickly quelled.[25]

The regiment was then ordered on October 9 to New Orleans, from where it moved west to the Berwick-Brashear City area just off the Louisiana coast. It was felt that the Union might try an invasion through Atchafalaya Bay.[26] This area was an important terminal point for blockade runners who brought supplies from Texas. In addition, any Union occupation in that locale would present an immediate threat militarily to central Louisiana.[27] Leaving for the area on November 1, the regiment was again split up on arrival and detachments were posted at various stations. Wingfield's company was assigned to Fort Chene on the Bayou Chene.[28] As in Mississippi, the duties were routine and tranquil and it is likely that many soldiers were disappointed that they had not yet seen the enemy.

When Fort Donelson in Tennessee fell to the Union troops of General Ulysses S. Grant in February, 1862, forcing Confederate forces under General Albert Sidney Johnston into a major withdrawal, the Fourth Regiment was among a number of units immediately ordered north to reinforce Johnston's army. On February 22, the regiment arrived in New Orleans and stayed for several days in an old cotton press. The troops then boarded trains and arrived in Jackson, Mississippi, on March 1 during a severe blizzard. In snow ten inches deep, the regiment camped at the local fairgrounds for approximately three weeks. During this time, Colonel Barrow resigned command of the regiment and Colonel Henry Allen was elected to succeed him.

In a freezing rain, the regiment again boarded trains on March 21 and was moved to Corinth, Mississippi, a small village just south of the Tennessee line, about ninety-two miles east of Memphis, arriving the next afternoon. An important railroad junction, Corinth had been heavily fortified by Johnston as a base for Confederate operations in the area. The Fourth pitched its tents on high ground outside of town near a spring and set to work building new fortifications. Joining regiments hastily called from other farflung points of the Confederacy, the troops set to the tasks of digging trenches, knocking down trees, and constructing ground obstacles, such as sharp branches slanted in the direction of the enemy, all intended to slow any assault.[29] To date, it was one of the largest Confederate forces assembled, however, most of the soldiers were new and untried in battle.[30]

Because Grant's forces around the Shiloh church in Tennessee, north of Corinth, were approximately the same in number as his, General Johnston decided to launch his forty thousand troops at Corinth in a major assault. It was critical that Grant be attacked before his army could be joined by that of Major General Don Carlos Buell, which was then advancing from Nashville. Marching in torrential rains, the Fourth and other units moved twelve miles north to Monterey, Tennessee, then to the Shiloh area. Swollen creeks slowed the advance and Johnston's schedule was delayed. To maintain the advantage of surprise, the troops were ordered to avoid loud noises, which was often ignored, and were not permitted to light any fires to ward off the cold. Finally, Johnston's army was in place on the evening of April 5. The Fourth was scheduled to be in the second line of attack under the command of General Braxton Bragg. At last, the eager troops of the Fourth were to taste the glory of combat for the first time, and one can imagine the apprehension each felt as he awaited the dawn. Early Sunday morning, April 6, Johnston's force attacked at Shiloh, completely surprising Grant and his army. Union defenses were initially weak and, in spite of the death of General Johnston as the result of a chance shot during the fighting, the Union forces were on the verge of defeat by the end of the day. The New Confederate commander, Beauregard, broke off the battle to reorganize his command for a decisive attack the next day.

In its first battle, the Fourth began its advance under the deafening explosions of Confederate artillery to the rear. A major on horseback captured a federal flag and wrapped it around his body. Waving his saber, he cheered the troops to

The Early Years 19

Eugene Bunch fought with the Fourth Regiment of the Confederacy at Vicksburg and Baton Rouge during the summer of 1862.

"come on." Unfortunately, his uniform was bluer than the normal Confederate blue grey. Nervous soldiers to the front of the unit mistook him for a Union soldier and riddled him with musket shot.[31] As a result, a nearby Tennessee regiment then confused the Fourth for Union forces and opened fire, killing and wounding twenty-seven men. Only after considerable confusion were commanders able to restore order and resume the advance. At about 1:30 P.M., the reorganized Fourth was ordered to move forward again.

Coming out of some thick underbrush, the troops found themselves the target of withering fire from Union forces only fifty feet away. The regiment immediately fell back, then mounted an attack which failed. General Bragg sharply directed Colonel Allen that "no flinching was wanted now." Embarrassed, a more resolute Fourth Regiment made another assault and again moved within fifty feet of the Union positions under heavy fire. The Thirteenth Louisiana Regiment helped out by flanking the Union position and the combined pressure forced the defenders to quickly fall back. The Fourth pursued them until it was halted at about 4 P.M., then began to withdraw from the battlefield.[32]

That evening, Grant's depleted and battered forces received the welcome reinforcements of General Buell and, when battle resumed at daybreak on April 7, the Confederates were subsequently forced to yield to the superior numbers. The Fourth had already withdrawn and started its return to Corinth. Both armies suffered heavy losses at Shiloh, totaling approximately twenty-four thousand troops. In its first battle, the Fourth had lost twenty-four killed and 169 wounded.[33] Most of the soldiers had lost their romantic notions of war amidst the noise and confusion of the battlefield. Both Eugene and T. C. had undergone a baptism of fire, exposed to the vivid reality of fear, blood, and death.

The regiment moved back to Monterey on April 9 to help cover the Confederate withdrawal to Corinth. On April 16, while returning to Corinth, the troops camped on a hillside near Ten Mile Creek. A Union Cavalry unit appeared, but after a brief skirmish, was driven back.[34] The regiment then rested for several weeks at Corinth.

Union forces occupied New Orleans on May 1. The next day, the Fourth was ordered to Edwards Station, Mississippi, just east of Vicksburg, to reorganize under General Bragg's Army of the Mississippi. Bunch's company was converted to Company E, Ninth Battalion, Louisiana Partisan Rangers, still under Wingfield's command.

The regiment was moved early in June to Vicksburg to help construct new fortifications. While the unit was there, the town was subjected to the Union's "First Seige," a naval bombardment that did little damage. During the same month, Baton Rouge was occupied by Union forces moving up from New Orleans and the town was held with the support of transports and gunboats on the Mississippi River. Confederate General John C. Breckinridge was assigned a four thousand-man detachment, including the Fourth, to attempt to recapture the city.

The detachment left Vicksburg on July 27, 1862, for Camp Moore, where a false rumor quickly spread that Union forces would be attacking there. Recontrol of Baton Rouge would give Southern forces another major control point on the Mississippi River to help protect the badly-needed Red River supply route. The Confederates could then even consider the retaking of New Orleans.[35]

As part of the Confederate strategy, the gunboat *Arkansas* was to confront the Union ships at Baton Rouge, coinciding its assault with that of Breckinridge's force. Giving the gunboat time to reach Baton Rouge, the troops remained at Camp Moore where the heat and summer rains resulted in widespread sickness. On August 3, with assurance that the 165-foot armor-plated ram boat was well on its way, Breckinridge led a two-day forced march to Greenwell Springs on the Comite River, ten miles east of Baton Rouge. Many soldiers had no shoes, while others had no shirt or wore only rags. Carrying full packs in the intense heat, thirsty men broke ranks to drink from stagnant pools of water along the roadside, only to fall out later with dysentery. Arriving at Greenwell Springs on the afternoon of August 4, a messenger brought word that the *Arkansas* would arrive early the next morning to join the attack. Breckinridge now had only 2,600 physically able but exhausted men who were to go into battle.[36]

That night, some 200 Partisan Rangers were posted to the rear of artillery units on various roads leading to Baton Rouge. Curious and impetuous, some imprudently moved too close in the darkness and inadvertently engaged Union pickets. The cavalry units fell back quickly to Confederate lines where, in the darkness and confusion, they were mistaken for the enemy and the resulting gunfire killed a lieutenant and wounded several men.[37] An alerted enemy was now prepared for the coming attack and defensive positions were strengthened, as well as the river gunboats being lined up.

At dawn, organized into two divisions, the Confederate force slowly advanced on Baton Rouge through a dense fog. The Fourth Regiment was assigned to the division under Brigadier General Daniel Ruggles, with Colonel Allen commanding the Second Brigade under Ruggles. Pressing its attack, the Confederates began pushing the Union troops back at the center of the defensive line into the city. On the left flank, however, they were not as successful. Colonel Allen led his men in a charge across a 300-yard open field against heavy infantry and artillery fire. When Allen fell seriously wounded, troops of his regiment removed him on a stretcher of muskets, the entire brigade at the same time falling back, confused and demoralized. A concentration of Union artillery fire hindered the efforts of commanders to reorganize the brigade and, in spite of Confederate advances on other flanks, the Second Brigade continued to retreat.

The badly-needed *Arkansas*, because of frequent stops for repairs, never made it to Baton Rouge in time. Breckinridge pulled his troops back east of the city to await the gunboat while Union forces, also in disarray, clustered by the river. Four miles north of the city, Union gunboats met the oncoming *Arkansas* and the resulting fight forced the rebel gunboat's crew to abandon it to subsequent destruction. As a result, Breckinridge decided not to renew the assault and withdrew further to the Comite River. He had lost eighty-four dead, 315 wounded, and fifty-seven missing, while the Northern forces suffered eighty-four dead, 266 wounded, and thirty-four captured or missing. Content to retain control of Baton Rouge, the Union forces did not attempt any pursuit of the retreating Southerners.[38]

After two weeks of waiting for a second Confederate assault, however, the Union command decided to evacuate and relinquish control of Baton Rouge, returning to New Orleans.[39] On August 13, Breckinridge's troops returned and moved into the city to set up a garrison. Shortly after this, on August 26, Ruggle's division, including the Fourth Regiment, was ordered to Port Hudson, on the Mississippi River twenty-two miles north of Baton Rouge, to begin construction of fortifications. For Eugene Bunch and his comrades, already hardened by combat, Port Hudson would prove an even sterner challenge. At home, symbolic of a key issue of the war, Bunch's father had sold an eighteen-year old Negro slave, Judy, and her son for $1,400 on February 24, 1863.[40]

NOTES

1. Bright Ray, *Legends of the Red River Valley* (San Antonio: The Naylor Company, 1941), pp. 68-79.
2. Letter to the author from E. Q. Richards, Macon, Mississippi, December 8, 1980.
3. Lucille Simms Mallon, *Noxubee County, Mississippi, Marriages, 1834-1869* (Noxubee County, Mississippi: Lucille Simms Mallon, 1975), book A, p. 53.
4. E. Q. Richards, "Deeds of Gift or 'Love and Affection,' 1834-1869," *Mississippi Genealogical Exchange*, Vol. 25 (Spring 1979), p. 26.

5. Deed Records, Noxubee County, Mississippi, Vol. E, p. 208; Vol. G, p. 406; Vol. J, pp. 276, 320; Vol. K, p. 26.
6. Letter from E. Q. Richards.
7. Texas State Archives, "Widow's Application for a Pension" (Flavia H. Bunch), book 7, no. 50758, May 16, 1932; Succession Book, Tangipahoa Parish, Louisiana, Vol. 1, p. 514.
8. Bunch's gravestone carries this as his date of birth, although exactly who had the stone erected after his death is obscure. Contemporary newspaper accounts at the time of his notoriety alleged that he was born in 1841. Census information from 1850 to 1880 is not totally adequate, but does lend credence to the 1843 date. During the probating of his mother's estate in August, 1875, his age was listed as 32 years.
9. Seventh U.S. Census, 1850, Noxubee County, Mississippi, p. 231; Succession Book, Tangipahoa Parish, Vol. 1, p. 514.
10. Record of Wills, Chancery Clerk, Noxubee County, Mississippi, Vol. 1, p. 144.
11. Letter from E. Q. Richards.
12. Deed Record, Noxubee County, Mississippi, Vol. K, p. 565.
13. Conveyance Book, Tangipahoa Parish, Louisiana, Vol. 5, p. 78.
14. Prentiss B. Carter, "The History of Washington Parish, Louisiana, as Compiled from the Records and Traditions," *Louisiana Historical Quarterly*, Vol. 14, No. 1 (January 1931), p. 52.
15. Eighth U. S. Census, 1860, Washington Parish, Louisiana, p. 16.
16. Napier Bartlett, *Military Record of Louisiana* (reprint ed., Baton Rouge: Louisiana State University Press, 1964), p. 241.
17. John D. Winters, *The Civil War in Louisiana* (Baton Rouge: Louisiana State University Press, 1963), p. 22.
18. John Smith Kendall, "Recollections of a Confederate Soldier," *Louisiana Historical Quarterly*, Vol. 29, No. 4 (October 1946), pp. 1048-1049.
19. John Smith Kendall, "Muster Rolls of the Fourth Louisiana Regiment of Volunteers, CSA," *Louisiana Historical Quarterly*, Vol. 30, No. 2 (April 1947), p. 504; National Archives and Records Service, "Index to Compiled Service Records of Confederate Soldiers who Served in Organizations from the State of Louisiana."
20. Bartlett, *Military Record*, p. 242.
21. Bartlett, *Military Record*, p. 247.
22. Robert Patrick, *Reluctant Rebel*, ed. by F. Jay Taylor (Baton Rouge: Louisiana State University Press, 1959), p. 32.
23. Kendall, "Recollections," p. 1052.
24. Kendall, "Recollections," p. 1053.
25. Sarah A. Dorsey, *Recollections of Henry Watkins Allen* (New

York: M. Doolady, 1866), pp. 54-55.
26. Kendall, "Recollections," p. 1053.
27. Patrick, *Reluctant Rebel*, p. 33.
28. Kendall, "Recollections," p. 1054.
29. Kendall, "Recollections," p. 1055-57.
30. Dorsey, *Allen*, p. 71.
31. Dorsey, *Allen*, pp. 77-78.
32. Kendall, "Recollections," pp. 1063-67.
33. *Confederate Military History*, Vol. X (Atlanta: Confederate Publishing Company, 1899), p. 170.
34. Kendall, "Recollections," pp. 1071-72.
35. Winters, *Civil War*, p. 111.
36. Winters, *Civil War*, p. 111-12.
37. Kendall, "Recollections," p. 1083; Dorsey, *Allen*, p. 134. The lieutenant killed was named Todd, a brother of President Lincoln's wife.
38. Winters, *Civil War*, pp. 119-22. Colonel Allen, after recovering from his wounds, subsequently became the Confederate governor of Louisiana.
39. Winters, *Civil War*, p. 123.
40. Property Transfer Book, St. Helena Parish, Louisiana, Book R, p. 474.

2 The Civil War

Located along the bluffs on the east bank of a curve in the Mississippi River, heavy artillery batteries at Port Hudson, at some points as high as eighty-five feet above the water line, gave the Confederates commanding domination of the river. As one observer stated, Port Hudson had a "capacity for offensive annoyance to the enemy."[1] A critical element of Northern strategy was control of the Mississippi Valley, which meant that both Vicksburg and Port Hudson had to be in Union hands.[2] The Confederates, however, depended heavily on control of the river to insure delivery of badly needed supplies. With the defeat of Confederate forces in this theater of operations, cotton and other crops would be diverted to the North.[3] More important, Union capture of Vicksburg and Port Hudson would mean that the western Confederate states would be cut off and a new western front could spell the defeat of the main body of Southern forces east of the Mississippi.[4]

General Grant, committed to opening up the Mississippi from the north, began planning his strategy in December, 1862, focusing his attention on Vicksburg. At the same time, Confederate defenses were completed at Port Hudson, General Franklin Gardner replacing Ruggles as commander. Life for the troops at Port Hudson was quiet and routine: reveille, inspections, drill, and parades. There were ample supplies of beef, sugar, molasses, salt, and corn meal.[5] By March, 1863, the number of troops assigned had steadily increased and Gardner organized them into four brigades.[6]

Union General Nathaniel P. Banks, responsible for moving up the Mississippi from the south to eventually link up with Grant, was looking for a possible bayou route that would allow him to move his forces around Port Hudson. However, Admiral David Farragut, whose naval forces had been a key element in the occupation of New Orleans, learned that some Union gunboats had been captured north of Port Hudson and decided that his ships would have to run the Port Hudson batteries in order to reach and destroy those gunboats before they could be turned to Confederate advantage. Farragut believed that, once past Port Hudson, his naval forces would then be able to blockade the Red River supply route as well as control the 150-mile segment of the Mississippi between Vicksburg and Port Hudson. Banks agreed to make a diversionary infantry move to distract Port Hudson troops while Farragut attempted to sneak his warships beneath the Confederate batteries.[7]

With twelve thousand troops under his command, Banks set up positions five to ten miles from the Port Hudson fortifications on March 13, 1863. On orders reflecting Banks' overestimate of Confederate strength, Union cavalry elements gingerly avoided contact with probing Confederate cavalry trying to lure them closer. Banks had no intention of becoming involved in a full engagement and, likewise, Gardner was not interested in leaving the secure Port Hudson defenses for any battle with Banks. The Union forces camped for the night,[8] expecting to make a diversionary movement at dawn to coincide with the movement of Farragut's ships.

At 10 P.M. that night, however, hours in advance of schedule, Farragut unexplainedly attempted to move his fleet beneath the Confederate positions. Gardner's artillery was alert and poured it on the slow-moving flotilla. A bonfire set by the Confederates on the opposite shore of the river illuminated the ships, making them highly visible. Of seven ships, only two successfully ran the batteries. After the three-hour battle, the Confederates had suffered only two minor casualties while the

Union forces had seventy-five killed or missing and thirty-five wounded.[9] Banks' troops returned to the south without making any attack.

Life at Port Hudson resumed its former routine with only an occasional minor skirmish for excitement. In addition to pastimes such as drills and inspections, almost every unit in the Confederate camp now had a crude brewery producing corn beer. Nearby planters, stuck with surplus sugar, readily provided this important ingredient to the popular "Louisiana Rum," even though Gardner regularly sent out details to destroy the distilleries and confiscate the brew. Two handwritten newspapers circulated each day throughout the camp, largely poking fun at officers. Those soldiers fortunate enough to have horses, mostly staff officers, attended various social activities in nearby local communities. Soldiers who had to remain in camp generally contented themselves with the music of a self-taught fiddler, if one happened to be assigned to their unit.[10]

By the end of March, 1863, Gardner commanded approximately sixteen thousand troops, organized into five brigades. Early in May, with no apparent threat of attack on Port Hudson, he was ordered to send five thousand troops north to Vicksburg to help face the pending Union attack by Grant's army. At the same time, Union Colonel Benjamin Grierson's nine hundred and fifty cavalry troopers had been enjoying tremendous success as they moved unobstructed through Mississippi into Louisiana, disrupting Confederate communications and transportation. Gardner sent out infantry, cavalry, and artillery detachments to intercept the raiders, but they missed them. Upon failing to intercept Grierson, a portion of these detachments, including elements of the Fourth Regiment, were ordered to join General Joseph Johnston's army at Jackson, Mississippi, to help in the effort to relieve Vicksburg.[11] Wingfield's cavalry unit, however, including Bunch and his brother, was left at Port Hudson.

Admiral Farragut's ships bombarded the Port Hudson de-

General Ulysses S. Grant, commanding general of the Union Army.

fenses on May 8 and 9, a bombardment that was to continue spasmodically into June. Gardner had built up a store of supplies, including cattle, sheep, and corn, against the possibility of a long-term defense. However, as Grant began maneuvering to mount his assault against Vicksburg, a panicky Confederate command ordered all troops at Port Hudson evacuated and moved to Jackson. General Banks' forces, however, had already moved into position around Port Hudson. It was too late; Port Hudson was surrounded. On May 22, elements of Wingfield's cavalry skirmished with advance forces of Banks' army, but fell back.[12] On May 25, Gardner refused Banks' request to surrender. The battle for Port Hudson was under way.

Beginning with a heavy artillery bombardment, Banks launched his men in a major assault on May 27. After furious fighting, the Union forces were finally driven back with heavy casualties: 293 killed, 1,545 wounded, and 157 missing. The Confederates lost 235 dead, wounded or missing.[13] At one point in the battle, fifteen men from Wingfield's battalion helped a Mississippi unit stand off an assault by a Negro unit, the first major confrontation between white and black troops in the war. The next day, while under a white flag to tend to the wounded and dead littering the battlefield, Banks violated the truce by fortifying his advance positions and improving gun enplacements.[14] The Union forces were about twenty-five to twenty-seven thousand strong, but Banks, smarting under the bloody repulse, decided to change his tactics and mount a steady seige, gradually advancing on Port Hudson by constructing and pushing forward portable barricades and by tunneling beneath Confederate gun enplacements.

During the next several weeks, as the Union army stepped up its campaign, both sides relentlessly improved their positions. But the strain was beginning to show on Confederate resolve. Colonel W. R. Miles, brigade commander on the Confederate right, was forced to place a guard on the Partisan Rangers of the Ninth Louisiana Battalion because, while on outpost or picket duty, some of them began to desert to the Union side.[15] There is no record, however, that Bunch or his brother made any such attempt with other members of their unit.

Union forces initiated another heavy bombardment on June 10. Banks was frustrated that the seige approach was taking too long. Learning from deserters that Gardner's troops were in worse shape than he expected, with only about a five-day supply of food left, he demanded on the 13th that Gardner surrender. The Confederate commander again refused.

The next day, in a dense fog, the batteries of the Union river fleet and those on land opened fire simultaneously. Infantry units used the thick smoke of the artillery to cover their attack along the line. Grenades were flung over Confederate parapets by the attacking soldiers, only to be thrown or rolled back at them. Shot and shell flew furiously between the opposing armies. After two hours, the Union forces were again pushed back with heavy losses: 203 dead, 1,401 wounded, and 188 missing, compared to the Confederates' rather modest twenty-two killed and twenty-five wounded.[16]

The Union seige was, however, beginning to tell on the embattled greycoats. As a result of more accurate shelling, those troops of the Fourth Regiment who remained at Port Hudson constructed a fifteen-foot deep hole, roofed with logs and earth, that they dubbed the "Gopher Hole," and in which they were safe from all but a direct hit.[17] Union snipers were also a continuing hazard and soldiers were careful to stay low when near the breastworks overlooking the river or at other defensive positions. The hot Louisiana sun, combined with shortages in food and ammunition, added to the strain. Heat exhaustion, dysentery, sunstroke, and malaria began to affect both armies. The Confederates had no more quinine or other medicines and operations and amputations had to be performed without the benefit of anesthetic. Gardner placed his troops on half-rations to forestall total depletion of food stocks.

Incredibly, after the June 14 assault, Banks coldly refused to allow removal of the dead from the battlefield around Port Hudson and, by June 17, the stench from decomposing bodies was overwhelming. Gardner finally raised a flag of truce on his own initiative and Confederate troops delivered enemy bodies to the Union side for burial.[18] An informal truce broke out between the two sides at various points along the line and soldiers on both sides openly improved their positions in full view of the enemy, occasionally exchanging banter and even small amounts of coffee, tobacco, newspapers, and sugar. Although Confederate commanders discouraged the fraternizing, the shortage of ammunition made the respite welcome. At other points on the line, however, deadly sharpshooting and nighttime raids continued.[19] Overall, though, there was a general lull in the intensity of combat between the two armies.

By the first of July, Confederate beef supplies at Port Hudson were gone and the men were forced to begin slaughtering mules and horses for food. Some soldiers even exhibited a preference for the large wharf rats that infested the camp. Depleted corn stocks were replaced by hard, indigestible cowpeas, which the troops refused to eat. There were still adequate stocks of sugar and molasses, which led the men to brew a crude beer that was preferable to the putrid water that was their only alternative. A sort of "coffee" was made from various parched supplies, such as wheat, rye, or meal, while those supplies lasted. The desire for tobacco was partially satisfied by smoking or chewing on leaves, vines, or bark.[20]

Union forces continued to tunnel under Port Hudson so that explosives could be planted beneath Confederate positions. At the same time, offensive barricades inched closer and closer to the Confederate lines, behind which sharpshooters would be shielded. Periodic bombardments and minor infantry probes also continued, further eroding the already tenuous Southern defenses.

With the failure of General Joe Johnston to come to the rescue, the Confederate force at Vicksburg finally surrendered to Grant on July 4 after an extended seige. Grant began preparations to send immediate assistance to Banks at Port Hudson. When word reached Port Hudson on July 7 that Vicksburg had fallen, Gardner knew he could no longer hold out. After verification of Vicksburg's surrender, a cease-fire was quickly arranged and, while commanders of both sides worked out surrender terms, Northern and Southern troops abandoned their positions to swap combat tales and supplies. Gardner prolonged the talks somewhat to allow time for those troops that could to escape through Union lines.[21] The Confederates had lost a total of 188 killed, approximately 200 dead from sickness, and 483 wounded. Banks lost 752 killed, 226 mortally wounded, 3,228 wounded, and 418 captured or missing.[22]

At 7 A. M. on July 9, 1863, with Bunch, his brother, and other battered Confederate soldiers lined up, Gardner formally surrendered to Banks in a simple ceremony. Earlier in the war, the North and the South had agreed to a system of swapping prisoners in order to avoid problems of extended housing and feeding. Where there was not an equal number, surplus prisoners would be paroled with the understanding that they could not be returned to combat duty until there was a formal notice of exchange.[23] Banks decided to parole the enlisted men but hold the officers until an exchange could be worked out later. On July 12, Eugene and T. C. Bunch were among about six thousand ragged soldiers paroled and allowed to return to their homes.[24] The prisoners struck off individually in all directions and Gardner's army "dissolved like a snowball in a thaw."[25]

Because Gardner was a prisoner himself, he did not have the legal authority to approve the paroles and the Confederate government later declared the action null and void, ordering all enlisted men paroled at both Vicksburg and Port Hudson to report to various reorganization points by September 15 for return to active duty.[26] Union authorities claimed this violated the rules that the two sides had agreed to, but at this stage of the war, the cumbersome system of prisoner exchanges and paroles had irretrievably broken down.

Formal military records on Eugene and T. C. Bunch end with their parole at Port Hudson in 1863. There is no information that they ever returned to the war which, by now, had turned badly against the South and finally concluded with Robert E. Lee's surrender to Grant at Appomattox on April 9, 1865. As to Bunch's performance as a Confederate soldier, the only information that can be located is in questionable newspaper accounts about him almost thirty years later. One account described him as a color bearer, selected because of his height, strength, and bearing. It indicated that he was wounded once in the head and once in the body. Another account, allegedly obtained from one of Bunch's extremely close friends in Texas, stated that he was never wounded during the war.[27] A third account made a dubious effort to connect his wartime experiences with his later notoriety:

> Bunch proved to be a good soldier and gave many evidences of that bravery approaching almost to desperation which marked his career in life. While not exactly of a quarrelsome disposition, he was quick tempered and became involved in many quarrels and fights with his comrades, but nothing serious ever came from these little differences. He contracted some bad habits, however, during the campaign around Port Hudson, Baton Rouge and eastern Louisiana, among which was a passion for gambling and drinking.[28]

Bunch's wife, when making application for a Confederate widow's pension in 1932, stated that he received an injury "in active service from which he never fully recovered," but she did not specifically identify the injury.[29]

After the fall of Port Hudson, stragglers, deserters, and

paroled prisoners roamed throughout the wooded parishes of Eastern Louisiana. These wartime renegades, rather than returning to Confederate duty, victimized citizens and openly dealt with Union forces foraging in the area. In addition, those Confederate soldiers still in service who remained in the area were scattered, demoralized, and also openly conversed with the enemy.[30] Whether or not Eugene Bunch was part of this rabble or returned to military service and combat is not recorded. If he was involved in the life of a brigand, it could have been a taste of the life he would pursue several decades later.

NOTES

1. *Confederate Military History*, p. 73.
2. Edward Cunningham, *The Port Hudson Campaign* (Baton Rouge: Louisiana State University Press, 1963), p. xii.
3. Cunningham, *Port Hudson*, p. 4.
4. Bruce Catton, *Never Call Retreat* (New York: Doubleday & Co., Inc., 1965), p. 4.
5. Cunningham, *Port Hudson*, p. 14.
6. Cunningham, *Port Hudson*, p. 21.
7. Winters, *Civil War*, p. 214.
8. Winters, *Civil War*, p. 215-16.
9. Cunningham, *Port Hudson*, p. 33.
10. Winters, *Civil War*, p. 219.
11. Patrick, *Reluctant Rebel*, p. 111; Kendall, "Recollections," p. 1107.
12. Cunningham, *Port Hudson*, pp. 44-45.
13. Winters, *Civil War*, p. 260.
14. Winters, *Civil War*, p. 260.
15. Winters, *Civil War*, p. 266.
16. Winters, *Civil War*, p. 274.
17. Cunningham, *Port Hudson*, p. 72.
18. Cunningham, *Port Hudson*, p. 96.
19. Winters, *Civil War*, p. 276.
20. Winters, *Civil War*, p. 280.
21. Cunningham, *Port Hudson*, p. 119.
22. Cunningham, *Port Hudson*, p. 121.
23. Bruce Catton, *Grant Takes Command* (Boston: Little, Brown & Company, 1968), pp. 370-71.

24. Andrew B. Booth, *Records of Louisiana Confederate Soldiers and Commands*, Vol. II (New Orleans: Louisiana Military Records Commission, 1920), p. 179; U. S. National Archives, "Index to Compiled Records."

25. Kendall, "Recollections," p. 1132. Lieutenant Colonel Wingfield, with other Confederate officers, was sent to New Orleans by steamship and hospitalized. He later was released on parole and escaped to rejoin the war.

26. Cunningham, *Port Hudson*, p. 120.

27. *New Orleans Daily Picayune*, November 13, 1888; *Gainesville* (Texas) *Daily Hesperian*, November 29, 1888.

28. *New Orleans Daily Picayune*, August 23, 1892.

29. Texas State Archives, "Widow's Application for a Pension," No. 50758 (Flavia Bunch).

30. Winters, *Civil War*, p. 307.

3 Gone to Texas

For the years immediately following the Civil War, there is little record of the activities of Eugene Bunch. James Bunch again moved his family, this time from Washington Parish to east of Amite City in neighboring Tangipahoa Parish where they were described as "highly esteemed and respected."[1] Eugene Bunch reportedly went to New Orleans and "attended a commercial school for a short time,"[2] then apparently returned to Amite City where he became a rural school teacher.

While there is no indication that Bunch received more than an average education for the times, he was bright and probably a good student. More than likely, he was well able to handle the job of teaching the basics to children of Amite City. A teaching position was often available to anyone who could read, write, and perform simple ciphers. However, after he became a notorious public figure over twenty years later, one press account dramatically attemped to paint him as a dissolute failure:

> His habits mitigated against his success as a pedagogue and soon his dissipation became known and, as usual in a small country town, became common talk. He was deposed, and for a time matters went from bad to worse. He became a confirmed drunkard and was soon an object of pity or contempt.[3]

It was even alleged that he taught his pupils to play poker rather than the "rudiments of learning."[4]

One of Bunch's pupils was a boy named Joseph Leon Pounds, who would allegedly succeed him as teacher. Pounds, who was born in Washington Parish on February 27, 1850, lived in the northwestern section of the parish with his parents and eight sisters. He later described his teacher as being highly respected.[5] In 1888, a leading Alexandria, Louisiana, merchant, J. D. Warren recalled that both he and Pounds were students of Bunch at a school at Pleasant Valley in Washington Parish. Warren stated that both Bunch and Pounds boarded with his father, W. C. Warren, who lived about two miles from the school. He described Bunch as a "fine looking and polished man and well liked by all."[6]

The newspaper's attempt to picture Bunch as a gambler and a drunk at this point in his life cannot be borne out with any available facts. The descriptions by his former pupils, if accurate, refute that image. In all likelihood, as often happened in contemporary newspaper stories concerning notorious characters, the reporter took considerable liberties with the facts to spin a story that fit his own fanciful notions. Other areas of Bunch's life were also cast by newspapers in a negative light to paint him as tragically flawed and a hopeless candidate for the outlaw trail. As another indication that this was not accurate, Bunch applied to join the Masonic lodge at Franklinton, but was subsequently admitted as a member to the lodge at Amite City.[7]

In 1869, tragedy struck when his older brother, T. C., with whom he had shared the privations of Port Hudson, died at the age of 28, probably of consumption. A member and officer of the Masonic lodge at Franklinton, T. C. had served as clerk of the Washington Parish Court in 1868.[8] In the next several years, Bunch's father, mother, and several of James Bunch's children would die of consumption and Bunch reportedly believed that it would also be the cause of his own demise.[9]

Eugene Bunch as a young man, although the time and place of the photograph is unknown. (Courtesy of Mrs. Zuma F. Magee.)

Sometime in the late 1860's, Bunch met Flavia H. Flynn, the daughter of Isaac T. "Ike" Flynn, a prominent planter in East Feliciana Parish. Flynn, then in his late forties, and his wife, formerly Amanda Pipes, had four daughters.[10] The planter had been quite wealthy prior to the Civil War, at one time owning 1,500 acres of land and sixty-two slaves.[11] Even though the Civil War had changed the circumstances of many formerly wealthy people in the South, there is an indication that Flynn may have retained some degree of his former prosperity after the war.

The tall, slim, auburn-haired schoolteacher must have made a distinct impression on young Flavia, who had been born in Clinton, Louisiana, on August 5, 1846.[12] After a courtship, the two were married in East Feliciana Parish on December 22, 1869.[13] It was later alleged that Bunch and his bride were given a $20,000 dowry by Flavia's father,[14] which Bunch supposedly squandered away over the next several years. It is hard to imagine, though, that Ike Flynn would make such a large gift, if he did, to any son-in-law who had a terrible reputation as a drunkard, gambler, and wastrel. This is another indication that, if the dowry story is true, Bunch was considered a suitable husband for Flavia, not a dissolute.

On July 21, 1870, the U. S. census taker listed Ike and Amanda Flynn as living in East Feliciana Parish with four daughters. Curiously, Flavia Bunch was shown as living by herself in the "household" next to Flynn's. Four days later, however, she was listed a second time as living with her husband of seven months in Washington Parish. Still a school teacher, Eugene and Flavia boarded in the home of Susan Faulke and her two domestic servants. The census also showed his parents, James and Martha, as living near Amite City in Tangipahoa Parish with eight children still at home.[15] However, on January 25, 1870, Martha had been granted a default divorce judgment. Her husband was able to get the judgment temporarily set aside in order to file an answer. However, Martha was awarded a divorce on February 8, 1870, and the court granted her 220 acres and a considerable cash settlement, including two mules, forty hogs, and twenty-six cattle.[16] Shortly thereafter, a judgment was returned in a separate matter against Martha for $526, apparently for a debt.[17] Perhaps James' restlessness of spirit had contributed to the breakdown in the marriage.

For some reason, Bunch became dissatisfied with what he was doing and felt the urge to move on. Throughout his life, people observed that he was seldom satisfied with a meager income, such as he was currently earning as a school teacher. Perhaps this could be traced to his early environment of comfort in Mississippi. The influence of his father's restlessness may have been another factor. Looking for something new, he chose Texas as the place to make a new life for himself and his wife. Just why he selected Texas and when he moved is not clear. Later newspaper accounts estimated that he moved sometime between 1870 and 1873.[18] In her application to the State of Texas for a Confederate widow's pension in 1932, an 85-year old Flavia declared that she had been a bona fide resident of the state since January 1, 1874.[19] However, her divorce petition, filed in May, 1889, claimed they came to Texas in 1871.[20]

Bunch and his wife left Louisiana and made the long trek across the blacklands of North Texas, finally stopping in the remote, rural town of Dexter in the far northeastern corner of Cooke County, about four miles from the Red River and the border between Texas and the Indian Territory. Dexter, which was named for a famous trotting horse of the era, has some notoriety as a distributing point for whiskey sold illegally to Indians in the territory just across the river.[21] Incorporated in 1874, the town has a population of about 300 people. Of the thirty-five business buildings in Dexter, seven were saloons and another seven were drug stores where, it was said, better liquor could be obtained with a prescription.[22]

Cooke County, in 1870, had an overall population of 5,315. With the coming of the railroad, however, the number of residents would increase in ten years to 20,391.[23] Basically a farming area, the county produced cotton, corn, wheat, oats, sorghum, and other grains.[24]

Once settled in Dexter, Bunch reportedly taught school for a while in conjunction with another teacher, Alex J. Thompson. In addition, he also did some farming with his younger brother, James, who had been born in approximately 1857,[25] but whose movements are not well documented. The first official record of Bunch in Texas was his purchase of a quarter-acre lot on Dexter's Main Street for $200 from J. R. Washington on November 21, 1874.[26] In the following month, he bought an additional six acres in Dexter for $180 from Elijah and Elizabeth Meador.[27] During this same year, Bunch's mother died in Louisiana, his father having died earlier.[28]

Bunch first showed up on the Cooke County tax rolls for 1875 and was credited with six acres and a lot worth a combined value of $370, $250 cash in hand, and miscellaneous property worth ninety-five dollars, for total taxable assets of $615.[29] Later that same year, he sold the Dexter lot to Margaret S. Taylor for $200.[30] As further evidence of some prosperity, he loaned Bayles O. C. Pound $200, payable at three-and-a-half percent per month interest and due a year later.[31]

In August, 1875, Flavia gave birth to a son, Theodore C., likely named after Bunch's brother.[32] T. C., as he would be called, was the only child that would result from their marriage.

As he established himself in Cooke County, Bunch began to gain more and more respect and entertained the idea of political office. On February 15, 1876, he was elected the County Clerk, although he apparently did not take office until May. The county's current election records do not go back any further than 1884, so it is impossible to determine who his opponents were or the amount of popular vote he accumulated. On May 29, Bunch was first mentioned in Commissioners Court minutes as performing the duties of County Clerk.[33]

Because there was currently no courthouse in Gainesville,

the county seat, the previous courthouse having burned, the county government was renting rooms around town for court sessions and offices. At the time Bunch was elected, court functions were being carried out in the upper storeroom of a local merchant.[34] On May 30, however, the County Commissioners rented a room in the "Weaver Office" for $5.33-1/3 per month as an office for the County Clerk.[35] Bunch had barely gotten his offices set up for business, however, when the Commissioners in August ordered him to remove his office "at once" to the south room of the County Jail.[36] Strangely, this would be the only circumstance to place Bunch involuntarily inside a jail during his life. The County Clerk oversaw all of Cooke County's records: deeds, marriages, probate matters, Commissioners Court minutes, elections, and other papers. Bunch was generally credited with doing an outstanding job and keeping the office's affairs in good order. Occasionally he would take trips to Dallas some thirty-five miles away for such official business as getting County books bound.

Bunch's assessable property in 1876 increased to a worth of $1,355, including two horses and two cows.[37] He made a continued effort in 1877 to improve his financial lot. In January, he borrowed $600 from J. H. Weaver, putting up all of his property as security, in order to buy three acres from a widow, Katie Queen, for $1,300. This land was located one-half mile north of Gainesville on Elm Creek. In July, he also purchased the interest left by Mrs. Queen's late husband in a Gainesville grocery store. In October, he bought another acre of land adjoining the three-acre tract.[38] The tax rolls for 1877 credited him with ten acres, one horse, two cows, four hogs, and other property, all assessed at $1,720.[39]

In the same year, James F. Lilly moved to Texas. Lilly had been born in New Orleans in July, 1842, and was raised and educated there. He had entered a military school, but when the war broke out, he joined the Washington Artillery as a gunner and first saw combat at the first battle of Manassas. Never wounded, he served throughout the war with distinction. He was part of the military escort that accompanied Jefferson Davis and his cabinet south at the end of the war. Davis personally discharged Lilly from Confederate service and shook his hand. He returned to New Orleans, then went to Biloxi, Mississippi, as a school teacher. On March 11, 1967, he married Bunch's sister, Laura, and divided his interests between Biloxi and Amite City. Laura bore him two children, James Bunch Lilly and Martha (Mattie) Caroline Lilly, before she died in July, 1872.[40] Lilly then married another of Bunch's sisters, Mrs. Mary C. Spring, in Amite City on October 13, 1873,[41] but she died childless the following year. When Martha Bunch died in 1874, he acted as administrator of her estate on behalf of his own two children by Laura, his wife, Mary, and the other six surviving Bunch children: Eugene, Cora, Luella, James, Ida, and Martha Eva.[42] When Lilly came to Texas with his children in 1877, he settled first in Gainesville, then moved east to Sherman where he worked for a year as a bookkeeper in a wholesale business. He returned to Gainesville in 1878 and Bunch appointed him as his Deputy Clerk.[43] He and his children boarded with the Bunch family.

Bunch continued to prosper in 1878. The tax rolls credited him with assets of $1,465, as well as being responsible for 431 acres for another person.[44] On May 8, he traded his six acres in Dexter along with $1,000 to R. B. and Margaret M. Sigler for two 160-acre tracts of land, one fourteen miles west of the town of Denton in neighboring Denton County, and one fourteen miles northeast of Fort Worth in Tarrant County.[45] Peter K. Mathews had died in Tarrant County in June, 1869, leaving his wife Margaret, and their children the land as part of his estate.[46] Margaret subsequently married R. B. Sigler in February, 1876. The Siglers sold the two tracts to Bunch on the condition that, should for some reason title to any portion of the land revert to the Mathews children, Bunch would retain possession of at least an equal portion.[47]

Sam Bass committed the first train robberies ever experienced in Texas. No doubt Bass' exploits were closely followed by Bunch. (Courtesy of the Rose Collection.)

46 The Train Robbing Bunch

His career as County Clerk seemed to be as successful as his real estate investments. In June, 1878, the County Commissioners finally contracted for the construction of the county's third courthouse.[48] Bunch was re-elected on November 5, 1878, to his second term. A. J. Thompson, his former teaching colleague, was elected the County Tax Assessor and Collector.[49] Bunch posted an official bond of $2,000 with four sureties: R. S. Rollins, Charles M. McClain, James W. Hayes, and E. F. Morris.[50]

During the first part of 1878, outlaw Sam Bass committed the first train robberies ever experienced in the State of Texas. Inside two months, Bass and his gang held up four trains around Dallas, generating a massive manhunt that ranged for months across North Texas, including Cooke County. That summer, after some narrow escapes from local posses and groups of Texas Rangers, Bass and his men moved south to their destiny at Round Rock, just north of Austin. The Rangers, kept informed of Bass' movements by a member of the gang, were able to engage the outlaws in a gun battle during which Bass was fatally wounded. The newspapers and general public comment at the time centered around the latest exploits of the Bass gang and the posses pursuing them. No doubt, Bunch was as interested in this news as other citizens caught up in the daring deeds of the colorful outlaw. Railroads were not particularly popular with many people of the time because of rather stronghanded methods in acquiring land right-of-way.

Bunch's financial dealings leveled off during 1879. He bought a cemetery lot in the Cooke County Cemetery for ten dollars. In May, he sold one acre out of the four he owned north of Gainesville. He bought the entire cotton crop of B. O. C. Pound in June for $250, even though it was still growing on Pound's farm twelve miles northeast of Gainesville, to be gathered and delivered by Pound.[51] For the year, Bunch had taxable assets of $1,492. On the eve of the 1880's, it seemed that Eugene Bunch was making a mark in Cooke County and taking his place as a prominent and respected member of the community.

By 1880, Bunch was head of a considerable household. In addition to Flavia and young T. C., two of his sisters, 24-year old Luella and 19-year old Ida, were living with him. James Lilly, his two young children, and a young niece were also boarding with the Bunch family, as well as Lilly's brother-in-law, attorney D. E. Barrett.[52] Perhaps this gave rise to the later legend of numerous relatives looking to him for support.

On July 12, 1880, Bunch filed suit in the Cooke County District Court against the Mathews children to remove the cloud from the title to the two 160-acre tracts he had purchased from the Siglers and to partition the land between him and the children. It was now being asserted that the land was community property acquired during the marriage of Peter and Margaret Mathews and that the children were entitled to half of the land. Bunch countered that, if the children did have a legitimate interest, he was entitled to 13/24 of the land.[53] In August, a local attorney was appointed by the court to represent the interests of the minor Mathews children. The suit was continued until March 8, 1881, when the court awarded Bunch an undivided 13/24 of the two tracts.

A court-appointed commission, W. W. Bobo, D. C. Bosen, and H. E. Valentine,[54] recommended a partitioning of the land. The court ordered that Bunch receive title to seventy-six acres in Tarrant County and eighty-seven acres in Denton County, the children to receive title to the remainder.[55] Bunch had already agreed to sell the seventy-six acres in Tarrant County, pending the partitioning, to a Mrs. F. A. Wright in April for $450. In addition, for forty dollars, he purchased a one-fifth interest in the acreage retained by the Mathews children in Tarrant and Denton Counties.[56]

The year 1880 was a good one for Bunch. His brother, James, showed up once again in Cooke County. Bunch paid $500 and again bought another cotton crop from B. O. C.

Pound.⁵⁷ In the November 2 election, he was re-elected to his third term as County Clerk, handily defeating a "Greenbacker" candidate by a 1,400-vote margin.⁵⁸ J. R. Walker was appointed Bunch's Deputy Clerk, J. F. Lilly having been elected the District Clerk. Bunch posted his $2,000 official bond through three sureties: J. M. Culp, C. G. Graham, and W. L. Fletcher.⁵⁹ In December, he paid J. N. Day $48.50 for a 450-pound bale of cotton, to be delivered to him on the public square in Gainesville.⁶⁰

Even though he won the Mathews suit, the image of respectable public official apparently began to erode for Bunch in 1881. In February, B. C. Kirtley had replaced Walker as Deputy County Clerk. Then, on March 26, without any recorded explanation, the minutes of the County Commissioners contained this entry: "It is ordered by the court that E. F. Bunch be cited to appear before the honorable Commissioners Court on the 8th day of April A. D. 1881 to show cause if any he can why he should not give additional security on his official bond." On April 8, Bunch appeared as directed and the Commissioners approved an additional bond of an unmentioned amount through the addition as sureties of former County Sheriff M. M. Ozment, County Judge T. J. Hall, E. F. Morris, M. G. Salmin, James W. Hayes, and F. B. Cleaves.⁶¹

Flaws in Bunch's character were beginning to catch up with him. Several years later it would be alleged that he embezzled county funds to make land transactions and to keep himself solvent.⁶² There is no record to substantiate that allegation. Certainly, the actions of the Commissioners indicate that some sort of official impropriety or something of a disturbing nature had been discovered, although apparently not sufficiently serious enough to force his resignation or warrant criminal charges. Perhaps the best clue as to what was happening to Bunch at this time was contained in a local assessment of him written seven years later when he was suspected of being a train robber:

Bunch's mania for gambling was his ruin. From the time he entered the army, all through the war and in the years that followed it was his ruling passion. He would play incessantly at any game of chance that was offered and the earnings of his labor were squandered with a recklessness that demoralized his whole life, led to his downfall politically and perhaps to crime, if the charges against him are true. Up to the time he left this country gambling was almost his only vice, though even then he had come to be regarded as a libertine. He was strictly temperate, never indulging in intoxicants of any character at any time. He never used tobacco in any form and it was only upon rare occasion that he was ever heard to utter an oath.[63]

Bunch's passion for gambling and perhaps the fluctuating state of his personal financial affairs may have worried the Commissioners to the point that they felt the need to better protect the county government. It would also be later alleged that, prior to coming to Gainesville, Bunch had reformed from a drinking habit. It was even claimed that he won his popularity and subsequent election as County Clerk by squandering his wife's storied dowry through gambling and abundant generosity.[64] Since the local newspaper was probably being quite conservative about Bunch, as he still had many friends in the area and there was no desire to embarrass them, the references to his passion for gambling and his reputation as a philanderer were remarkably candid. The writer even pointed out that "his domestic relations were unpleasant almost from the first of his married life."[65] No doubt, Bunch's lifestyle and the rumors floating around, so typical of a small town, made the Commissioners quite uneasy.

In spite of his problems, however, Bunch still tried to make a go of it. In April, 1881, he bought a lot in Gainesville when it was auctioned off for unpaid taxes.[66] In August, William Wantland became his Deputy Clerk, followed in November by Harry Jackson.[67] Acting as a real estate agent in December, Bunch was given power of attorney by B. C. Rhone of neighboring Wise County to sell some land for him.[68]

In February, 1882, he and Flavia gave a lien on their three-acre homestead on Elm Creek just north of Gainesville to Waples, Painter and Company as security for a promissory note in the amount of $332.13. The money went for lumber and materials to make improvements on their home and land. Waples, Painter and Company dealt in "lumber, sash, doors, blinds, shingles, lime, cement, plaster, and hair," as well as the "best ready-mixed paints."[69] Bunch agreed to pay the note by June 1, 1882, with ten per cent annual interest from the date of the note. In that same month, his brother, James, became the latest Deputy County Clerk. Two months later, in April, he paid farmer M. V. Phipps $290 to buy back the original six acres in Dexter that he had traded to Margaret Sigler in 1878. Curiously, she had sold it to Phipps in February, 1880, for $850. Perhaps gambler Bunch filled an inside straight for a change, a conceivable explanation for the apparent bargain. By June, brother James was no longer signing any official documents as Deputy Clerk.[70]

Waples, Painter and Company grew impatient when Bunch did not pay his February debt to them. The business filed suit against him in District Court on July 17, 1882. The merchants told the court that, although Bunch and his wife had been requested numerous times to meet the terms of the note, the firm had been paid nothing. They asked for a judgment on the $332.13 loan plus interest. In addition, the court was petitioned to foreclose on the three acres Bunch had posted as security.[71] On August 11, Bunch and his wife failed to appear in court and the plaintiffs were awarded $349.60. The court foreclosed on the land and ordered it sold by the County Sheriff to satisfy the debt and court costs. The firm subsequently received payment in full on the debt on November 28, 1882.[72] Although no record could be found as to whether or not the land was sold, Bunch and his wife apparently managed to retain control of the three acres, perhaps through the assistance of family friends. The county tax rolls continued to show him in possession of the three acres.

Bunch began, however, to steadily divest himself of his assets, apparently to meet growing debts. In September, 1882, he sold 16-4/5 acres, his one-fifth interest in the Mathews children's Tarrant County property, to W. W. Bobo, who originally helped to partition it, for a modest eighty-four dollars.[73] In October, he and Flavia sold the six acres he had bought in April from farmer Phipps to Henry Gatewood for $600.[74] He did not run for re-election on November 7, 1882, his reputation as a gambler and ladies man now probably too much of a political liability. He made his last official signature as Clerk on November 20[75] and yielded the office to the newly-elected Clerk, A. J. Thompson. It had all begun to come apart for Eugene Bunch.

NOTES

1. *New Orleans Daily Picayune*, November 13, 1888. The Washington Parish Courthouse burned completely in 1897, destroying valuable records of Bunch's presence there.
2. Gainesville (Texas) *Daily Hesperian*, November 29, 1888.
3. *New Orleans Daily Picayune*, August 23, 1892.
4. *New Orleans Daily Picayune*, November 15, 1888.
5. *Bogalusa* (Louisiana) *Daily News*, August 13, 1953.
6. *New Orleans Daily Picayune*, November 15, 1888.
7. Letter to the author from Mrs. Zuma F. Magee, Franklinton, Louisiana, January 15, 1981.
8. Zuma F. Magee, *The Eugene F. Bunch Story*, unpublished manuscript (Franklinton, Louisiana: Zuma F. Magee, 1975), p. 6.
9. *New Orleans Daily Picayune*, August 23, 1892.
10. Eighth U. S. Census, 1860, East Feliciana Parish, Louisiana.
11. Joseph Karl Menn, *The Large Slaveholders of Louisiana, 1860* (New Orleans: Pelican Publishing Co., 1964), p. 219.

12. Texas State Archives, "Widow's Application for a Pension," No. 50758 (Flavia Bunch). Her death certificate gives a date of birth of August 1, 1845. Bureau of Vital Statistics, State of Texas, Death Certificate No. 1734, Dallas County, June 7, 1936.

13. Texas State Archives, "Widow's Application for a Pension," No. 50758 (Flavia Bunch).

14. *New Orleans Daily Picayune*, August 23, 1892.

15. Ninth U. S. Census, 1870, Tangipahoa Parish, Louisiana, p. 35; East Feliciana Parish, Louisiana, p. 298; Washington Parish, Louisiana, p. 8.

16. Minute Book, Tangipahoa Parish, Louisiana, Vol. 1, pp. 47, 75, 78-79; Conveyance Book, Tangipahoa Parish, Louisiana, Vol. 2, p. 78.

17. Minute Book, Tangipahoa Parish, Louisiana, Vol. 1, p. 123.

18. *Gainesville* (Texas) *Daily Hesperian*, November 29, 1888; *New Orleans Daily Picayune*, November 13, 1888.

19. Texas State Archives, "Widow's Application."

20. 44th District Court Records, Dallas County, Texas, cause no. 7431, May 30, 1889.

21. C. N. Jones, *Early Days in Cooke County* (Gainesville, Texas: C. N. Jones, 1936), p. 10.

22. Jones, *Early Days*, p. 83.

23. *Texas: Cooke County, Its People, Productions and Resources* (Gainesville: Cooke County Immigration Society, 1888-1889), p. 6.

24. *Texas: Cooke County* (Gainesville: Cooke County Immigration Society, 1888-1889), p. 3.

25. *Gainesville* (Texas) *Daily Hesperian*, November 29, 1888. It is interesting to note that one of Bunch's fellow privates in Wingfield's company was an A. J. Thompson, although there is no information that they were the same person. If they were, it could be one explanation of Bunch's choice of Dexter as a new home in Texas. Kendall, "Muster Rolls," p. 504.

26. Deed Record, Cooke County, Texas Vol. 11, p. 543.

27. Deed Record, Cooke County, Texas Vol. 11, p. 541.

28. Succession Book, Tangipahoa Parish, Louisiana, Vol. 1, p. 514.

29. Tax Records, Cooke County, Texas, 1875.

30. Deed Record, Cooke County, Texas, Vol. 12, p. 62.

31. Deed Record, Cooke County Texas, Vol. 13, p. 53. Another coincidence is the presence in Cooke County of several families named Pound or Pounds. There is no information connecting these families with Bunch's former pupil in Amite City, Louisiana, although conceivably, as with A. J. Thompson, they may represent another link between Cooke County and Louisiana.

32. Twelfth U. S. Census, 1900, Montague County, Texas.

33. Minutes, County and Commissioners Court, Cooke County,

Texas, Vol. 1, May 29, 1876. Minutes of the meeting of the Commissioners Court just previous to this meeting are missing and probably reflected Bunch's official bond being posted.

34. A. Morton Smith, *The First 100 Years in Cooke County* (San Antonio: The Naylor Co., 1955), pp. 63-64.

35. Minutes, County and Commissioners Court, Cooke County, Texas, Vol. 1, May 30, 1876.

36. Minutes, County and Commissioners Court, Cooke County, Texas, Vol. 1, August 29, 1876.

37. Tax Records, Cooke County, Texas, 1876.

38. Deed Record, Cooke County, Texas, Vol. 14, pp. 62, 96, and 546; Vol. 15, p. 371.

39. Tax Records, Cooke County, Texas, 1877.

40. *Biographical Souvenir of the State of Texas* (Chicago; F. A. Battey & Co., 1889), pp. 524-25. Lilly later married Mary H. Pipes, daughter of John H. Pipes of Cooke County. Curiously, Pipes was the maiden name of Flavia Bunch's mother.

41. *Tangipahoa Democrat*, October 17, 1874; Marriage Record, Tangipahoa Parish, Louisiana, Vol. 1, p. 129.

42. Succession Book, Tangipahoa Parish, Louisiana, Vol. 1, p. 514.

43. *Biographical Souvenir*, pp. 524-525.

44. Tax Records, Cooke County, Texas, 1878.

45. Deed Record, Cooke County Texas, Vol. 19, p. 419; Deed Record, Denton County, Texas, Vol. J, p. 237; Deed Record, Tarrant County, Texas Vol. K, p. 125.

46. District Court Records, Cooke County, Texas, cause no. 1233, July 12, 1880.

47. Deed Record, Cooke County, Texas, Vol. 19, p. 419.

48. Jones, *Early Days*, p. 15. The courthouse would burn down in 1909.

49. Smith, *First 100 Years*, p. 236.

50. Minutes, County and Commissioners Court, Cooke County, Texas, Vol. 2, p. 222.

51. Deed Record, Cooke County, Texas, Vol. 17, p. 519; Vol. 32, p. 185; Vol. 18, p. 99.

52. Tenth U. S. Census, 1880, Cooke County, Texas, p. 227. The 1870 Census in Louisiana listed a Loula S., age 15, and Lou E. age 10, in the Bunch family, and the age would indicate that it was Luella who moved to Texas. There was no Ida listed with the family in 1870, the closest in age at that time being Eva M., age 5, who was actually Martha Eva. However, Ida Elisabeth was born about 1860.

53. District Court Records, Cooke County, Texas, cause no. 1233, July 12, 1880.

54. Civil Minutes, District Court, Cooke County, Texas, cause no. 1233, Vol. 4, p. 506. In February, 1881, Margaret Sigler had filed for divorce from R. B. Sigler, alleging that he had abandoned her in May, 1878, after squandering her property, failing to provide for her, and reducing her to poverty. Sigler denied this and the suit was later dismissed in February, 1882, when the two were believed to be living together again in Jack County.

55. Civil Minutes, District Court, Cooke County, Texas, cause no. 1233, Vol. 4, p. 523.

56. Deed Record, Tarrant County, Texas, Vol. U, p. 362; Vol. Z, p. 233.

57. Deed Record, Cooke County, Texas, Vol. 19, p. 572.

58. *Dallas Daily Herald*, November 9, 1880.

59. Minutes, County and Commissioners Court, Cooke County, Texas, Vol. 2, p. 513.

60. Deed Record, Cooke County, Texas, Vol. 20, p. 243.

61. Minutes, County and Commissioners Court, Cooke County, Texas, Vol. 2, pp. 523, 555-56.

62. *New Orleans Daily Picayune*, August 23, 1892.

63. *Gainesville* (Texas) *Daily Hesperian*, November 29, 1888.

64. *New Orleans Daily Picayune*, August 23, 1892.

65. *Gainesville* (Texas) *Daily Hesperian*, November 29, 1888.

66. Deed Record, Cooke County, Texas, Vol. 21, p. 171.

67. Minutes, County and Commisssioners Court, Cooke County, Texas, Vol. 3, pp. 9 and 49.

68. Deed Record, Cooke County, Texas, Vol. 24, p. 477.

69. Gainesville City Directory, 1887-1888, p. 5.

70. Deed Record, Cooke County, Texas, Vol. 23, pp. 352, 385, 569; Vol. 21, p. 455; Vol. 25, p. 51.

71. Clerk's File Docket, District Court, Cooke County, Texas, cause no. 1370, Vol. 1, p. 51.

72. Civil Minutes, District Court, Cooke County, Texas, cause no. 1370, Vol. 5, p. 212.

73. Deed Record, Tarrant County, Texas, Vol. 123, p. 288.

74. Deed Record, Cooke County, Texas, Vol. 28, p. 228.

75. Marriage Certificate Book, Cooke County, Texas, November 10, 1882.

4 Outlaw Beginnings

No longer in political office, Bunch was forced to look for some other means to provide for his family. Very likely, he was gambling even more and was quite a familiar face in the saloons of Dallas and Fort Worth. He still owned a little land and was also probably still able to borrow from friends. Likely, he also looked for occasional business as a real estate agent.

Suit was filed against Bunch on January 15, 1883, in the Cooke County District Court by R. B. Sigler for "trespass to try title."[1] Sigler alleged that, in February, 1880, he had been in lawful possession of the six acres in Dexter that his wife, Margaret, had sold that same month to farmer M. V. Phipps and which Bunch had briefly owned for a second time in 1882. According to Sigler, Bunch had "unlawfully entered upon and disposed plaintiff of said premises" and that he had "greatly damaged said premises by cutting timber therefrom and abusing and defacing the dwelling house thereon." Sigler asked the court for $250 in damages as well as $288 for rent due for occupancy of the house.

Apparently, Bunch was not in Cooke County at this time as he could not be located by the Sheriff to be served notice of the suit and the case had to be continued. Finally, on July 20, 1883, some six months later, he was located and served. On August 10, in response, Bunch filed a disclaimer with the court stating that he did not have any rights, title, claim, or interest in the land at the time alleged and that it had been conveyed to Phipps. He asked that he be discharged from the suit. On February 6, 1884, when Sigler failed to appear in court, the suit was dismissed.[2]

By December, 1883, Flavia's younger sister, Minerva, who was born in Louisiana on August 28, 1862, had moved to Cooke County and was probably living with the Bunch family. In that same month, Bunch and five others, E. F. Morris, J. W. Sacra, Isaac Cloud, A. J. Addington, and C. C. Rumrill, convinced Minerva to loan them $1,000 for some business scheme. They executed a promissory note to repay the loan in one year at twelve per cent interest. Addington and Sacra were reportedly from the Indian Territory.[3] Bunch was still divesting himself of assets, though, and, in February, 1884, sold a portion of the land he owned in Denton County to G. W. McSpadden of Wise County for $441.[4]

His brother, James, sought to become a property owner so that his family would have a place to live. In August, 1884, he bought a lot in Gainesville, giving Isaac Cloud ten dollars and signing two promissory notes for ninety-five dollars each. One note was payable in May, 1885, and the other in May, 1886.[5]

With the county elections coming up in November, Bunch apparently decided on another try for respectability and a regular income. He filed for the County Clerk's position and began his campaign. However, on November 2, 1884, according to Cooke County election records, A. J. Thompson garnered 2,565 votes to Bunch's 1,629 and was re-elected. Bunch's defeat was blamed directly on his passion for gambling.[6] Any future for him in Cooke County must have seemed quite dismal at this point. Reportedly, he had a quarrel with Flavia and left the county, only to return periodically after that.[7] This is consistent with reports of his deteriorating marriage and his repeated efforts to achieve financial success. Bunch moved on to Wichita Falls to try his luck there.

Texas Ranger Captain Sam McMurray suspected that Captain Eugene Bunch had been involved in several Texas train robberies near Fort Worth. (Courtesy of the Western History Collections, University of Oklahoma.)

The townsite of Wichita Falls had only been laid out as recently as 1876 in anticipation of the arrival of the railroad then being constructed from Dallas. There was not even a permanent settler in the town until 1879. Wichita County was formally organized in June, 1882, and the Fort Worth and Denver Railroad first arrived the following September. With cattle as the area's foremost industry, there were soon enough saloons constructed in booming Wichita Falls that local wags referred to the town as "Whiskey-Taw."[8] Such an environment certainly attracted those opportunists, gamblers, prostitutes, and others who followed the railroad to each new terminal point. Bunch may have been lured to Wichita Falls by that same attraction.

In 1883, the year Wichita Falls became the county seat, several newspapers were organized there. Beauregard Bryan founded the *Wichita Herald* and was in charge of it for about a year.[9] Bryan, in conjunction with partner A. D. Matheny, also did job printing of forms, stationary, and statements for the county government in addition to publishing the *Herald*.[10] On February 28, 1885, Bunch and Matheny, now the sole owner, signed an agreement whereby Bunch would edit the *Herald*, in return for which he was to receive one-half of the net profits of the company. In addition, Bunch would pay Matheny $650 out of those profits for half ownership of the *Herald*.[11]

A recent account of Bunch's life, drawn from old files of the Pinkerton's Detective Agency, stated that Bunch had posed as the editor of a Richmond, Virginia, newspaper and that he edited a "Texas newspaper" for six months, after which it folded. A second account, which actually only paraphrased the first, had Bunch editing the newspaper in Dallas. William Pinkerton wrote that he edited a Gainesville newspaper.[12] In actuality, the *Wichita Herald* continued to do business for many years after Bunch left Wichita Falls. Only a few years after he left, it was reported by a New Orleans newspaper that he conducted the *Herald* with a great deal of ability,[13] although there is no record of how long he edited the newspaper or whether or not he actually became a part owner. No copies of the newspaper have survived.

Bunch also reportedly opened a real estate agency in Wichita Falls and made a number of profitable deals.[14] On October 9, 1885, John W. Dobkins named him as his agent to dispose of various parcels of land he owned in Wichita County. On October 13, Herman Sprecht bought all of the land for $42,759.60, a tidy sum of money in those days. Sprecht paid $18,810.86 in cash and assumed responsibility for various of Dobkins' outstanding promissory notes.[15] It can probably be safely assumed that Bunch's fee for this transaction was a healthy one. He was described as a "sharp trader" and quite adept at getting the best of any real estate deal. One anonymous Dallas man would later mournfully recall that Bunch had gotten to him at Wichita Falls for $1,000.[16]

However, it was later alleged that Bunch was still continuing on the "downward track." His success apparently only further encouraged preoccupation with his vices. Reportedly, he remained at Wichita Falls for about two years, then sold his business interests profitably and moved to Fort Worth.[17] Beyond the newspaper agreement and the Dobkins land deal, there is no other official record of Bunch's presence in Wichita Falls.

For all practical purposes, Eugene Bunch had forsaken his family and seldom saw his wife and son. According to one source, after leaving for Wichita Falls he only returned to Gainesville for a day or so about once a year.[18] Flavia later alleged that he abandoned her and T. C. in March, 1886, although her sister, Minerva, would recall that it was in December, 1885.[19] Bunch made no provisions for the care of his family and left them in considerably slim circumstances.[20] Curiously, the Gainesville city directory for 1887-1888 listed Bunch as a real estate agent who lived in a residence at 304 South Denton Street at the corner of Church Street. His son, Theodore, was a clerk for M. H. Brown and lived with his father.[21] Perhaps there was an effort to keep up appearnaces for a short while.

Minerva Flynn bought James Bunch's Gainesville lot from him on February 18, 1886, for $500, paying him $276 in cash and assuming the two ninety-five dollar notes he owed Isaac Cloud on the original purchase.[22] In September, she sold the lot to J. F. Lilly.[23] When Minerva married Henry C. Wilkerson in November, the house in which Flavia and T. C. were living burned to the ground. Flavia received a small amount of insurance money and moved with her son to Dallas.[24] Apparently she had some assets since, on December 8, she loaned $500 to Charles P. Whiteman, a friend who had been present when she married Bunch and who now lived with his wife, Bertha, in San Diego, California.[25] Neither Flavia nor T. C. ever saw Eugene Bunch again.

The late 1880's saw the outbreak of a spate of train robberies in Texas that generated considerable public comment and exasperated and confounded law enforcement officials. Few of the bandits were ever caught. In December, 1886, three unmasked men held up the passengers of a Fort Worth and Denver train near Bellvue, in Clay County. On January 23, 1887, robbers held up the mail and express cars of a Texas and Pacific train near Gordon, sixty-eight miles west of Fort Worth. At about 2:30 A. M., a gang of about seven men piled rocks on the track. Two men who had climbed aboard the engine ordered the train halted, part of the train extending onto a bridge over Barton's creek. Shooting through the express car door, the outlaws forced the Pacific Express messenger to open the door. They got less than $2,000 as well as some registered mail. The Sheriff of Dallas County, Henry Lewis, was on the train and fired one shot at them out the window. He held his fire, however, when the bandits threatened the lives of the engineer and fireman.[26]

A posse went after the train robbers and it was later alleged that Bunch rode with it and subsequently brought two suspected men to Dallas County.[27] There is no information available, though, to verify this and it seems quite unlikely.

During this time, while ostensibly passing himself off as a real estate agent from Gainesville, Bunch was alternating between the gambling parlors of Dallas and Fort Worth, eking out an existence in the wide-open sections of both towns. Dallas, in a continuous conflict of community values, periodically cracked down on its saloons, variety theaters, and gambling parlors. November of 1886 was one of those periods and the police conducted regular raids, rounding up as many gamblers and "vagrants" as could be found. The county grand jury returned almost 500 indictments for saloons being open on Sundays.[28] Approximately twenty-five gamblers from Fort Worth, including the notorious Luke Short, were arrested on over 400 cases of gaming charged against them, but none appeared in court when required and forfeited their bonds. Bunch could very well have been one of the gamblers arrested, but no record as to their identity, other than that of Short, survives.[29] The gambling cases against Short were subsequently dismissed on February 25, 1887.[30]

The Dallas police crackdown on gambling during 1887 was such that, to enter a "gambling den," the prospective player would have to give a predesignated signal to get through a series of doors to where the action was. In the event of a raid, the delay in admitting the police gave the gamblers inside time to put on an innocent face.[31] Each October, when Dallas proudly hosted the State Fair, scores of swindlers, pickpockets, burglars, and gamblers flocked to the city. Every year, the local police added to the payroll a number of temporary officers to help with the crowds. Experienced detectives from major cities connected by railroad to Dallas, such as Houston, St. Louis, and Kansas City, were hired during the Fair to keep an eye out for con men they recognized as having come to Dallas from their respective cities.

In Fort Worth, the gamblers shared a similar relationship with their city as those in Dallas thirty miles to the east. The newspapers in both cities were critical of the existence of gambling, but privately, the vice was encouraged by those who enjoyed poker, faro, or keno and other delights of the red light districts. Quite often, payoffs to members of the local police relieved some of the pressure or, at least, provided for some advance notice of a scheduled raid.[32] Luke Short enjoyed the reputation as "Boss of Gambling" in Fort Worth, having come to the city with a well-known background of close association in Dodge City, Kansas, and other places with the likes of Wyatt Earp, Doc Holliday, and Bat Masterson. He was known to have killed at least one man in a barroom dispute. Short owned a third interest in the White Elephant Saloon on Fort Worth's Main Street and ran a grand upstairs gaming room with elegant carpets, drapes, and chandeliers. His operation was "uptown" and socially removed from the sleazier saloons and parlors near Fort Worth's stockyards.[33] Bunch circulated in this milieu and may even have been in Fort Worth on February 8, 1887, and witnessed the shooting death of Longhair Jim Courtright, Fort Worth's former marshal and a well-known gunfighter, at the hands of Luke Short.[34]

According to a description of Bunch several years later in a New Orleans newspaper, he was reputed to be an able, but unlucky gambler. In addition to poker, he played faro, monte, and other games, but was more frequently a loser than a winner. Often without any money, he hung around gambling houses and rubbed shoulders with fellow "tinhorns," from whom he occasionally borrowed money.[35] A dramatic assessment of him in a Fort Worth newspaper said:

> Bunch was a remarkable man. He was highly educated which, with his urbanity and generous nature made everyone his friend. He had a commanding, knightly appear-

Luke Short operated the White Elephant Saloon in Fort Worth during 1887 when Eugene Bunch was making the rounds as a gambler. (Courtesy of the Kansas Historical Society.)

ance and was universally thought to be a high-minded, honorable man. Though he was easy to become acquainted with, but few ever became intimately so. Those who were so distinguished noticed an abnormal restlessness about him and an eye that on occasion flashed death to whoever crossed him. He boasted to very intimate friends that he had not been without reach of a brace of pistols for ten years.[36]

Flavia's sister, Minerva, now Mrs. Henry Wilkerson of Dallas, filed suit on March 5, 1887, in the Cooke County District Court against Bunch and the five others she had loaned $1,000 in December, 1883. She asked the court's assistance in getting her money back. On April 13, Bunch waived issuance of all process, stating that he didn't even want a copy of her petition.[37] None of the defendants, including Bunch, appeared in court on April 29 and Minerva was awarded damages of $2,310 plus court costs.[38] There is no record, however, that she ever received a cent of the judgment.

In spite of his gambling failures, Bunch remained a sharp real estate man. He bought some tracts of land on May 18, in Fort Worth from W. H. Skinner for $13,500. He gave Skinner $500 in cash, title to $5,000 in real property located in Gainesville, and assumed four outstanding promissory notes owed by Skinner. The next day, Bunch sold the same tracts to R. E. Maddox for $5,500 in cash, Maddox also assuming Skinner's promissory notes. And on May 20, R. C. DeHaven sold Bunch a quit claim deed for ten dollars on a tract of land adjacent to that which he had purchased from Skinner.[39] How Bunch gained title to so much land in Gainesville, if indeed he really did, is not a matter of record. No criminal indictments or civil suits concerning the matter are on record, so it can only be assumed that the transaction was legitimate.

At 8:10 P. M. on June 4, 1887, the eastbound Texas and Pacific train from El Paso was boarded and stopped on a trestle over Mary's Creek two miles west of the small town of Benbrook, southwest of Fort Worth about ten miles. Four men quickly took control of the train. One man, his face blacked and wearing a red handkerchief over the lower part of his face, confronted the Pacific Express messenger and helped himself to $1,350 and registered letters from the mail car. The conductor frantically warned the passengers to hide their valuables, but the robbers never attempted to hold them up. When the robbers left, the passengers reportedly cheered. From Fort Worth, the Sheriff led a posse of eight men with bloodhounds to the scene while another group of lawmen attempted to head the bandits off, but without success.[40] Around Texas, law enforcement officers were instantly suspicious that strangers suddenly appearing in their communities may have committed the train robbery. Within a week of the holdup, Dallas City Marshal James C. Arnold and Deputy U. S. Marshal Ben Cabell arrested two different men for the robbery. One was even "positively identified" until he was luckily able to prove that he had been on jury duty in Austin when the robbery occurred.[41]

A week after the robbery, on June 11, Bunch bought a parcel of land in Fort Worth from R. L. Carlock for sixty dollars.[42] On July 25, however, he sold the remainder of his acreage in Denton County to M. C. Costen for $137.50.[43] In his last known transaction, on August 26, 1887, Bunch sold his three-acre "Bunch Homestead," less than a half-mile north of the Gainesville public square, to W. W. Howeth, a local real estate agent and partner with his father in an abstract and loan company. Howeth paid him $800 in cash and gave him a note for $800 payable on September 1, 1888.[44]

The Fort Worth area was confounded when, on September 20, 1887, robbers again held up the Texas and Pacific train at exactly the same spot near Benbrook as in June and in the same manner. The Fort Worth Daily Gazette wryly observed that the robbery did not cause much excitement since "a thing to be exciting must contain an element of novelty, and train robbing has become so very common, as to scarcely deserve any uncommon display of headlines in a newspaper." Two men had mounted the cab and, at pistol point, ordered the engineer to stop the train on the bridge over Mary's Creek. Two other bandits joined them and they went to the express car where, after the robbers shot throught the door and almost battered it down with some timber, the messenger opened up. Both the express and mail cars were rifled and the outlaws escaped with a sizeable amount of loot. A posse with bloodhounds scoured the area, finding only some campers who had earlier seen four likely suspects.[45] Again, strangers appearing in area towns were subjected to close law enforcement scrutiny.[46]

Three train robberies committed in the area within nine months without any apprehensions was a bitter pill for local law enforcement officials. Only nine years before, Sam Bass had made area officers look silly. The Texas governor was ready to commission hundreds of new Texas Rangers to guard trains all over the state.[47] However, after a similar train robbery at Genoa, Arkansas, in December, 1887, investigation led to the arrest of Will Brock, who gave a full confession. It was finally determined that the Bellvue and Fort Worth area robberies had been committed by the Rube Burrow gang, which included Rube, his brother Jim, Will Brock, Nep Thornton, and Henderson Bromley.[48]

Later newspaper accounts attempted to connect Bunch with the Burrow gang, some even confusing him for Will Brock. It was alleged that he was absent from Fort Worth when the robberies occurred and then showed up later flush with money for gambling. It was claimed that officers suspected Bunch at the time because of his unusual movements. When Bunch was first identified as a train robber in November, 1888, the United States Marshal in Dallas, William L. Cabell, a former Confederate general, declared that Bunch had been a suspect in the Fort Worth area train robberies months before, but that he and his deputies could not find any evidence in order that he could

U.S. Marshal William L. Cabell suspected Bunch of every train robbery in Texas. (Courtesy of the Texas Collection, Baylor University.)

be charged.⁴⁹

In connection with this, a story was later widely circulated claiming that Marshal Cabell, in October, 1887, ordered a deputy, Lum Johnson of Gainesville, to arrest Bunch as a suspect in the September Benbrook robbery. Johnson supposedly approached Bunch in Dallas' Glen Lea Saloon, somewhat apologetically, and told him he had to arrest him. Bunch is then supposed to have pulled a pistol on the hapless deputy and instructed him to report back that General Cabell and his whole staff could not arrest him. Johnson dutifully left to follow the instructions and Bunch reportedly stayed around Dallas for a week or so without any problems from the marshal.⁵⁰ When this story was printed shortly after Bunch was actually identified as a train robber late in 1888, Marshal Cabell vehemently denied that any warrant had ever been issued for Bunch's arrest or that an arrest was attempted,⁵¹ branding the story as false.

Despite the lack of verifiable connection between Eugene Bunch and Rube Burrow, the coincidence is too significant to be overlooked. As events would prove, there would be other coincidences that would cause their lives to parallel each other. The Fort Worth area robberies were consistent with the geographical and chronological presence of Bunch. Even though he was not involved, perhaps the apparent ease with which the bandits held up the trains and escaped with fairly good-sized hauls, not to mention the excitement and glamor attaching to such desperate deeds, made a significant impression on Bunch. It may have influenced him strongly to eventually try his own hand at it.

By early 1888, in order to fund his expensive gambling habit and the various women he regularly entertained, Bunch had begun forging deeds of trust or vendors lien notes. Using his ostensible occupation of real estate agent, he endorsed them over for cash to unsuspecting businessmen in Fort Worth and Dallas. Only when he was identified later in the year as a suspected train robber, however, would the forgeries come to light.

Three notes of $400 each were forged on the name of W. W. Howeth of Gainesville, two of which were passed in Dallas and the third in Fort Worth.⁵² Colonel O. Brewster, a Fort Worth capitalist, bought a note from Bunch for $750 and J. C. Laning, also of Fort Worth, bought three notes from him totaling $1,685.⁵³ Two phony notes worth $500 each were also put up by Bunch as security on a loan in Fort Worth using the name of a Wichita Falls businessman, George A. Soule. Another forged deed of trust on land in Wichita County involved two notes of $1,000 each and used the name of J. L. Pounds as the party to whom Bunch had allegedly sold the land.⁵⁴

Another forged note, allegedly given to Bunch by an "A. S. Yates" on an $800 loan, pledged 320 acres of land in Denton County as security and was dated March 12, 1888. Bunch endorsed the note over to the Fort Worth partnership of Harger and Calloway, probably at a "discount."⁵⁵

Commenting on the forgeries when they finally came to light in November, the Fort Worth *Daily Gazette* quoted an unnamed acquaintance of Bunch that "quite a quantity of paper was out in this city" and that it fully explained how he would be flat broke one day and then be flush with cash the next.⁵⁶ Bunch had now crossed the line and it only encouraged him to bigger and bolder acts.

But, before the forgeries came to light, he had not entirely lost all of his apparent respectability. A frequent visitor to Dallas in the spring of 1888, the presence of "E. T. Bunch" in the city was briefly noted in a newspaper on March 20.⁵⁷ It was also later reported that he served a full term on the federal grand jury in Dallas at this time.⁵⁸ A more likely account reported that he had served on a petit jury in the Dallas federal court, supposedly for the trial of an alleged train robber, but the accused had escaped and the trial was never held.⁵⁹

Sometime by 1887 or early 1888, Bunch met Mrs. Cora Littlehale. Formerly Cora N. Ellis, she was born in 1857 to Ira and Mary Ellis in Texas. Her father had come to Texas from

Kentucky in 1838, and, by 1850, had married and had one son. Ellis was a land trader and, in addition to building the first brick building in Tyler in 1851, ran a family grocery store on the town square as well as a grist mill.[60]

On April 15, 1875, Cora married Fred H. Littlehale in Tyler.[61] Her husband was a buyer of cotton, wool, and hides, and by 1884, he and his wife had moved to Dallas. However, by 1887, Cora and Fred were no longer living together and she worked as a compositor for the Western Newspaper Union in Dallas.[62] It was at this time that Bunch came into her life.

A later newspaper account described Cora as a "woman of attractive appearance, educated, and of good family, who had left her husband." In the same newspaper, however, it was stated that she had been led astray by Bunch and this conduct so upset her husband that he gave up his business. Another report described her as a "medium-sized, delicate-looking woman, not by any means what the world would call a beauty yet.... sufficiently attractive to enlist more than a passing thought from the gallant" Bunch. It was also claimed that she had been a variety actress at one time.[63] A more likely account stated that Fred Littlehale failed in business at Dallas and that he and Cora moved to Wichita Falls where they separated. Cora reportedly returned to Fort Worth, then to Dallas.[64] At some time during this period in one of these towns, she met Eugene Bunch and fell in love with him.

NOTES

1. Clerk's File Docket, District Court, Cooke County, Texas, cause no. 1411, Vol. 1, p. 60.
2. Civil Minutes, District Court, Cooke County, cause no. 1411, Vol. 5, pp. 410 and 507.
3. Clerk's File Docket, District Court, Cooke County, Texas, cause no. 3036, Vol. 2, p. 61.
4. Deed Record, Denton County, Texas, Vol. Z, p. 178.
5. Deed Record, Cooke County, Texas, Vol. 38, p. 66.

6. *Dallas Morning News*, November 18, 1888.
7. *Gainesville* (Texas) *Daily Hesperian*, November 29, 1888: *New Orleans Daily Picayune*, August 23, 1892.
8. Jonnie R. Morgan, *The History of Wichita Falls* (Wichita Falls, Texas: Nortex Offset Publications, Inc., 1971), pp. 16-49.
9. Frank W. Johnson, *A History of Texas and Texans* (Chicago: The American Historical Society, 1914), Vol. III, p. 1303.
10. Minutes, Commissioners Court, Wichita County, Texas, Vol. I, 1884-1888.
11. Deed Record, Wichita County, Texas, Vol. H, p. 523.
12. James D. Horan and Paul Sann, *Pictorial History of the Wild West* (New York: Bonanza Books, 1954), p. 147; Jay Robert Nash, *Bloodletters and Badmen* (New York: M. Evans and Co., Inc., 1973), p. 91; William A. Pinkerton, *Train Robberies and Train Robbers*, reprint of 1907 edition (Fort Davis, Texas: Frontier Book Co., 1968), p. 51. A letter from Mr. Horan to the author, January 10, 1981, explained that the original information on Bunch in the Pinkerton's files, which he examined in 1946, has since been misplaced or lost by the agency.
13. *New Orleans Daily Picayune*, August 23, 1892.
14. *New Orleans Daily Picayune*, August 23, 1892.
15. Deed Record, Wichita County, Texas, Vol. 1, pp. 248-50.
16. *New Orleans Daily Picayune*, August 23, 1892.
17. *New Orleans Daily Picayune*, August 23, 1892.
18. *Gainesville* (Texas) *Daily Hesperian*, November 29, 1888.
19. 44th District Court Records, Dallas County, Texas, cause no. 7431, May 30, 1889.
20. *Gainesville* (Texas) *Daily Hesperian*, November 29, 1888. The Dallas *Morning News*, on August 24, 1892, reported that "before leaving them he gave them all his possessions and did everything to ward off want." The Fort Worth *Gazette* of August 25 indicates the same thing, but this is most likely inaccurate.
21. Gainesville City Directory, 1887-1888, p. 54; Ed Bartholomew, *The Biographical Album of Western Gunfighters* (Houston: The Frontier Press of Texas, 1958), p. 12.
22. Deed Record, Cooke County, Texas, Vol. 38, p. 67.
23. Deed Record, Cooke County, Texas, Vol. 39, p. 370.
24. *Gainesville* (Texas) *Daily Hesperian*, November 29, 1888. A witness in Flavia's divorce action also asserted that she moved to Dallas in November, 1886.
25. Deed Record, Dallas County, Texas, Vol. 90, p. 131.
26. *Fort Worth Daily Gazette*, January 24, 1887.
27. *New Orleans Daily Picayune*, November 15, 1888.
28. *Dallas Morning News*, November 10, 1886.

29. *Dallas Morning News*, November 17-19, 1886.
30. *Dallas Morning News*, February 26, 1887.
31. *Dallas Daily Herald*, May 7, 1887.
32. William R. Cox, *Luke Short and His Era* (Garden City, New York: Doubleday & Company, Inc., 1961), p. 160.
33. Cox, *Luke Short*, pp. 156-159.
34. F. Stanley, *Longhair Jim Courtright* (Denver: World Press, Inc., 1957), p. 213.
35. *New Orleans Daily Picayune*, August 23, 1892.
36. *Fort Worth Gazette*, August 25, 1892.
37. Clerk's File Docket, District Court, Cooke County, Texas, cause no. 3036, Vol. 2, p. 61.
38. Civil Minutes, District Court, Cooke County, Texas, cause no. 3036, Vol. 7, p. 111.
39. Deed Record, Tarrant County, Texas, Vol. 47, pp. 384, 386, and 400.
40. *Fort Worth Daily Gazette*, June 5, 1887.
41. *Dallas Morning News*, June 25, July 1, 1887; *Dallas Daily Herald*, June 25, 1887.
42. Deed Record, Tarrant County, Texas, Vol. 51, p. 354.
43. Deed Record, Denton County, Texas, Vol. 30, p. 506.
44. Deed Record, Cooke County, Texas, Vol. 43, p. 154.
45. *Fort Worth Daily Gazette*, September 21, 1887.
46. Paul Harvey, Jr., *Old Tige: General William L. Cabell, CSA* (Hillsboro, Texas: Hill Junior College, 1970), pp. 68-69. Dallas' U. S. Marshal William L. Cabell, at the request of the Parker County Sheriff who had four suspects, caused warrants to be issued and the men were brought to Dallas. After a pre-trial hearing in which the charges were dropped, one of the suspects, H. D. Arnold, sued Cabell and others for false arrest in August, 1888. Cabell was acquitted at the trial but, after Arnold appealed, Cabell was ordered to pay a total of $1,566.91 in damages and costs. See also *Cabell V. Arnold*, 23 S. W. 645 (Texas Ct. Civ. App. 1893).
47. Richard Dillon, *Wells, Fargo Detective* (New York: Coward-McCann, Inc., 1969), p. 236.
48. Carl W. Breihan, *Outlaws of the Old West* (New York: Signet Books, 1980), pp. 86-113; James D. Horan, *The Pinkertons* (New York: Bonanza Books, 1967), pp. 371-75.
49. *New Orleans Daily Picayune*, November 15, 1888.
50. *New Orleans Daily Picayune*, August 23, 1892.
51. *Dallas Morning News*, November 19, 1888.
52. *Gainesville* (Texas) *Daily Hesperian*, November 16, 1888.
53. *Gainesville* (Texas) *Daily Hesperian*, November 24, 1888.
54. *Gainesville* (Texas) *Daily Hesperian*, November 25, 1888.

Outalw Beginnings 73

Forging the name of "A.S. Yates" to this vendor's lien note, Bunch "discounted" this and other such notes to unsuspecting victims in Dallas and Fort Worth in order to finance his gambling activities.

55. Minutes, 17th District Court, Tarrant County, Texas, cause no. 4652, Vol. M, p. 626: Vol. O, p. 87; Vol. P, p. 75. Joel P. Harger and W. P. Calloway were in a brief partnership in Fort Worth during 1888 to trade and deal in wood and coal. Calloway, without Harger's knowledge or approval, bought the note from Bunch, then later discounted the note to Fort Worth banker John C. Harrison for $600 so that Calloway could immediately pay $400 to a railroad company for delivery of a load of coal. On November 21, 1888, Harrison brought suit against Bunch, A. S. Yates, and Harger and Calloway for $1,500 in damages. Bunch and Yates were subsequently dropped from the suit and, on December 30, 1890, after Harger had presented evidence of his innocence in the matter, the court found against Calloway only and ordered that he pay Harrison $1,175.68 plus interest and court costs, even though, originally, the note was forged. Harrison appealed the decision because Harger, not Calloway, was the only member of the partnership who had the means to pay such a settlement.

56. *Fort Worth Daily Gazette*, November 22, 1888.

57. *Dallas Morning News*, March 20, 1888.

58. *New Orleans Daily Picayune*, November 15, 1888.

59. *Dallas Morning News*, August 25, 1892.

60. Seventh U. S. Census, 1850, Smith County, Texas; Ninth U. S. Census, 1870, Smith County, Texas; Letter to the author from Ms. Jo Green, Library Clerk, Tyler, Texas, August 14, 1981.

61. General Index to Marriages, Smith County, Texas Vol. H, p. 16.

62. Dallas City Directory, 1884-1887.

63. *New Orleans Daily Picayune*, August 23, 1892; November 13, 1888. For some reason, the files of the Pinkertons also indicated a belief that she was the daughter of a former Texas governor, Horan and Sann, *Pictorial History*, p. 147. Tyler produced three governors, but Ike Ellis was not one of them.

64. *New Orleans Times-Democrat*, November 16, 1888.

5 Robbery in Louisiana

Eugene Bunch and Cora Ellis may have gone to New Orleans as early as December, 1887, according to one report.[1] Bunch had assumed the alias of J. H. Gerald and Cora posed as his wife. He supposedly stayed with her for a short while, then, when she was comfortably installed in a boarding house, returned to Texas. The trip to Louisiana could have given Bunch an opportunity to renew some old friendships, particularly that of his former student, Joseph Pounds, or J. Leon Pounds as he was now known. The use of "J. L. Pounds" on the forged deed of trust early in 1888 would seem to indicate that there already had been some contact between the two.

J. Leon Pounds lived with his wife and family about twenty-five miles northeast of Covington, near what is now the city of Bogalusa. A carpenter, blacksmith, and farmer, he occasionally even built coffins for neighbors. He also ran a logging operation that hauled logs by raft to a lumber mill in Pearlington, just north of where the Pearl River flowed into the Mississippi Sound.[2]

Bunch wrote a letter to Pounds from Dallas on June 8, 1888, advising him that he would be leaving for New Orleans and would be going under the name of Captain J. H. Gerald. Later it would be asserted that, while in Dallas, Bunch was "in communication with parties in Nashville. . .Cincinnati. . .Louisville. . .Fort Worth, and other towns in Texas, and also with a number of men whom the law said were at one time criminals,"[3] supposedly attempting to recruit them for some criminal enterprise. It may have been at this time that Cora accompanied him to Louisiana, rather than the previous December.

Sometime during this same period, Bunch also returned to Gainesville for a short visit. From the room where he was staying, he sent for local businessman W. W. Howeth. He told Howeth about the forgeries he had committed using the businessman's name and promised to settle the notes when they came due for payment.[4] As a model for the forged liens, Bunch had used the legitimate notes given him by Howeth as part payment for his three-acre homestead. Howeth would later remember his own nervousness when, upon entering the room, Bunch closed the door behind him and laid a six-shooter on the table while discussing his crimes, acting "almost like a madman."[5]

Another acquaintance Bunch had before he left Texas was the Dallas City Marshal, James C. Arnold. Arnold would later recall that Bunch was a "right jovial fellow" with a "droll voice." According to Arnold, when U. S. Marshal Cabell suspected Bunch as a culprit in the 1887 Fort Worth area train robberies, Bunch approached him on the street one day and greeted him, "Hello, Arnold. I understand they've got me down for a train robber." Shortly after that, Arnold said, he went by train to Fort Worth with Texas Ranger Captain McMurray and Ben Cabell, the son of the U. S. Marshal and who would become Dallas County Sheriff in 1892. At the train station, Arnold met Bunch and asked him if he was going to Fort Worth, to which Bunch replied that he was not. However, once they were aboard the train, Bunch entered their car and took a seat facing Cabell and McMurray and rode to Fort Worth. Although nothing happened, Arnold said that he was later told that Bunch had intended to kill McMurray, thinking that the Ranger was trying to trap him for the train robberies. Arnold never saw him again after this, having known him "a good while."[6]

Apparently, Bunch talked too much before he returned to New Orleans, discussing rather freely his criminal plans and ideas. Some person, probably a local gambler in whom Bunch confided, relayed the information to Marshal Arnold, even giving the officer copies of telegrams to verify the story. Arnold recalled one telegram which read something like: "The contract is let. If you are not here (by a certain time) it will be let to another," using the word "contract" to throw off suspicion.[7] Another acquaintance of Bunch would later anonymously claim that a Dallas gambler received a letter sent by Bunch from Louisiana proposing to rob a train near New Orleans. The gambler was then supposed to have "given the snap away" in hopes of a reward.[8]

Arnold notified railroad officials in Dallas, according to him, then went to New Orleans with the idea of heading off Bunch. Arnold left Dallas by train for New Orleans on August 22, 1888, to pick up a wanted fugitive who had been conveniently arrested there by local police. Sophus Atkinson had fled Dallas earlier in the month with some stolen hides and another man's wife. While awaiting requisition documents from the Texas governor, Arnold stayed over in New Orleans, finally returning with his prisoner to Dallas on August 28.[9] He had consulted with New Orleans Police Superintendent David C. Hennessy who assigned Detectives Gaster and Pecora to work with him. Arnold told them that Bunch was supposed to be going under the name of Gerald and staying with a woman on Carondelet Street. It was Arnold's feeling that it was only a matter of time before Bunch would attempt to rob a train.[10]

By June of 1888, "Captain Gerald" and his wife had been staying in a room at the fashionable boarding house of Mrs. Charles Hogan at 141 St. Charles Street, taking their meals at a restaurant rather than at Mrs. Hogan's. Mrs. Hogan would remember the pair as incongruous, Mrs. Gerald being petite and well-dressed while her husband was "slouchy and unclean in his

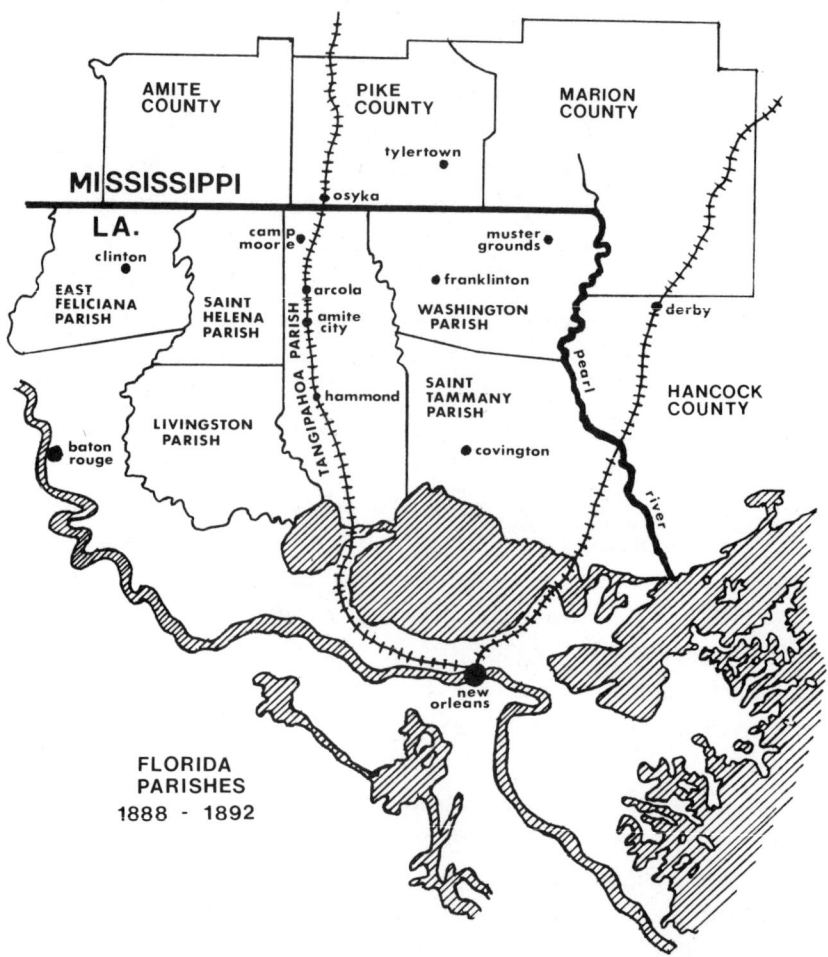

The area throughout which Captain Bunch and Rube Burrow were believed to have robbed trains.

Deputy U.S. Marshal Ben E. Cabell may have been a target of Bunch on a train ride to Ft. Worth. (Courtesy of The Texas Collection, Baylor University.)

Dallas Police Chief James C. Arnold was alerted to Bunch's suspicious activities and tried to thwart him in New Orleans. (Authors's Collection.)

apparel."[11] The Geralds also reportedly stayed at 191 Carandolet Street.[12] The New Orleans police had received a complaint from a man named McLendon that "Captain Gerald" had sent him a threatening postal card. Gaster and Pecora, after locating Gerald, sent a friend to warn him that he would be arrested if he sent any more threats. Gerald sent word back that McLendon had been "talking about him" and that, if McLendon would quit, he would quit, too. No further incident occurred between the two.[13] Apparently, this incident happened before Gerald's true identity had been revealed to the police.

Captain and Mrs. Gerald reportedly took little excursion trips from New Orleans, occasionally for several days at a time, to such nearby places as Bay St. Louis in Mississippi, Pearlington, Covington, and other places in St. Tammany, Washington, and Tangipahoa Parishes.[14] For a while, the two were under surveillance by New Orleans detectives and Bunch was observed occasionally leaving the city alone by train and lounging around depots and saloons in small towns along the railroad line, as well as in Covington. Newspapers later reported that the detectives had suspected the two were counterfeiting or "shoving the queer," a slang term for passing counterfeit money.[15] It may have been that, although it was suspected that Bunch was up to no good by Marshal Arnold and the New Orleans police, no one really had any idea what. Until Bunch did something illegal, they could not arrest him. More than likely, Bunch was at the time finalizing his plans, unaware that the police suspected anything.

At some point during this period, while visiting with Pounds, Bunch wrote Pounds a fictitious letter, dated November 1st and addressed from Vernon in the Indian Territory. The letter was personal in character, indicating that Bunch had arrived in Vernon safely and was in excellent health. Bunch gave the letter to Pounds and instructed him to keep it so that Bunch would have an alibi in case he or Pounds was arrested by detectives.[16]

Pounds subsequently paid Captain and Mrs. Gerald several visits in New Orleans. On the evening of October 18, 1888, he contacted them again and loaned his former teacher forty-two dollars.[17] Early in the morning of October 31, an explosion tore a large hole in the roof of an express car of the New Orleans and Northeastern Railway. The express messenger declared that someone had thrown dynamite on the train, but, since there had been no overt robbery attempt, an investigation of the matter was not made. It was subsequently speculated that Bunch may have slipped out of the city on the evening of October 31 and made an attempt to hold up the train.[18] It was also reported that on that same date, Bunch was seen meeting with Pounds near Covington.[19]

Before dawn on Saturday, November 3, 1888, train number five of the New Orleans and Northeastern Railway rolled southbound to New Orleans, having originated in Cincinnati, Ohio. Charles W. Lowrey, the messenger for the United States Express Company, shared the express car with the train's baggagemaster, Henry C. McElroy. The car was located between the tender to the locomotive and the train's second class smoking car. Lowrey worked at the front of the car, checking the freight and packages being sent to New Orleans, which included a large number of chicken coops stacked in rows. McElroy sat on a trunk toward the middle of the car, his back toward the rear door leading to the smoking car. This door was often left open to allow the conductor or other members of the train's crew to visit them.

Earlier that morning, just as the train had pulled out of Hattiesburg, Mississippi, the train's porter, Green Turner, thought he heard a noise on top of the express car and stopped to listen for a minute. Hearing nothing more than the sound of the train building speed in the darkness, he forgot about it and returned to his duties. The train moved on to a brief stop at Derby Station, still in Mississippi about sixty-four miles north of New Orleans, then started up again, soon attaining its usual speed of about forty miles an hour.

At about 4:20 A. M., McElroy was involved in writing and did not notice a man enter the car through the rear door, close it, and lock it from the inside. With a revolver pointed at him, the baggagemaster's thoughts were rudely interrupted by a harsh command to throw up his hands. McElroy looked up and saw a tall, thin, stoop-shouldered man wearing a black slouch hat, jeans trousers, a "seedy-looking" coat, and carrying two pistols. The man had a "florid" complexion and long red whiskers. A red bandana was tied around his neck and the ends were stuffed over his mouth and nose in an effort to disguise his voice and features. The baggagemaster hesitated and tried to set aside the paper on which he was writing, but the man cursed him and again ordered him to raise his hands and stand up. He turned McElroy around and, nudging him rudely in the back with a pistol, pushed him to the other end of the car.

Lowrey was busily checking the freight and was between two rows of chicken coops when he heard a hoarse, muffled voice. He turned and saw McElroy with a man standing behind him and what he at first thought were the mouth of a bottle and a revolver extended toward him over the baggagemaster's shoulders. The man gruffly commanded him to throw up his hands. Lowrey laughed and made a light reply, thinking that the train crew was playing a practical joke. But then he saw McElroy's wide eyes and pale face. The masked man swore at him, repeating his command and stabbing the air menacingly with his two pistols. Lowrey's hands bolted skyward and, at the bandit's direction, he and McElroy, both still facing each other, shuffled toward the express company's iron safe where they were ordered to get to their knees.

The bandit ordered Lowrey to open the safe. When the express messenger started to retrieve the key from his pocket, he was ordered to stop and the bandit told him that he knew him well and had been watching both of them for a long time.

"You're mistaken, partner. I've only been on the road since September," Lowrey replied.

The gunman again cursed him and told him to shut up. He reached over McElroy and took the safe key from Lowrey's pocket, then handed it to him and told him to open the safe, which he did.

The masked man removed four or five small white cotton bags from his trousers pockets and threw them to the floor, telling Lowrey to remove all the money from the safe and put it in the bags. Lowrey had managed to drop his own wallet, which contained fifteen dollars, to the floor without the robber seeing it. He began stuffing the contents of the safe into one of the bags. One sealed package in the safe contained $10,000 consigned to the Mutual National Bank in New Orleans. Lowrey asked the bandit if he wanted this package as it contained only broken watches and junk.

"Yes, put it all in there," the armed man replied, "and be damned quick about it or I'll blow the top of your head off."

However, as Lowrey picked up another bag, the robber changed his mind and told him to put one of the bags over McElroy's head. Doing as he was told, Lowrey then finished filling the second bag. Told to put a bag over his own head, the express messenger nervously pulled the bag on, the draw strings catching on his ears and nose. The irritated robber told him to hurry and Lowrey later recalled hearing one of the pistols being cocked near his head.

With a revolver nudging their stomachs, the two hooded men stood and were slowly backed up until the baggagemaster was seated on top of the safe and Lowrey was in a chair. The bandit told them, "Keep quiet or I'll blow your damned brains out." He then searched the safe one more time and cut open the mail pouch from Vicksburg, removing a number of letters and papers and scattering them over the floor of the car.

Preparing to leave, the masked intruder warned the two men that he would come back to find them if they talked about the robbery. He told them to say that he was a "low, chunky" man, rather than tall and slim. He then pulled the train's bell cord four times and, as the train obediently slowed to a stop, departed through the door at the front end of the car, just behind the tender, and jumped off the platform to the ground. The entire robbery had not taken more than fifteen minutes. A passenger in the smoking car looked out the window and, in the darkness, saw a man carrying what looked like two bags walk leisurely into the woods several hundred yards away.

When the train stopped, about a mile and a half north of Lacey's station at McClure's Switch, the conductor, brakeman, and porter checked through the length of the train to see what was wrong. Coming to the express car, they found the rear door locked and had to go around to the front of the car. Upon entering, they found the two men, still not sure the robber had left, cautiously pulling the bags from their heads. The train was again checked, but no passengers were missing and no one could recall seeing anyone who fit the description of the robber.

The train went on to New Orleans where the police were immediately notified. Since the robbery had occurred in Mississippi outside local police jurisdiction, the express company consulted Farrell and Boylan's Detective Bureau. Private detectives took a special train that evening for the scene of the robbery and began to search the area.[20]

In New Orleans, officials of the United States Express Company began trying to ascertain the loss. It was revealed that the robber had overlooked a wooden chest in a corner of the car which contained packages of money and other valuables, including the railroad's payroll, which had been too large for the safe. The initial estimate of the loss was approximately $30,000, including twenty bonds issued by the Fifth District Levee Board of Louisiana and valued at $1,000 each.[21]

The news of the train robbery excited the community and considerable comment was heard. As an example, the November 4 *Daily Picayune* lamented the meekness of the two victims:

> The lone highwayman, possibly the same rascal who has for years been in the habit of robbing railway trains and stage coaches in Texas has now transferred his operations to the railways in the neighborhood of this city. Yesterday morning he captured the express messenger and baggagemaster on the Northeastern train and had little or no trouble in securing large amounts of money in transit in the care of each. The robber was so successful, meeting not the slightest resistance from the two men who had charge of the money, that his exploit will invite other adventurous loafers who read dime novels to attempt similar crimes.
> Some time ago an express messenger in Texas, single-handed, fought a gang of robbers, killing one and saved his charge, but that was a rare case, one of the few on record. It is astonishing what one plucky villain can accomplish in overaweing and subduing men engaged in honest occupations. A criminal may be desperate and reckless, but an honest man with a good conscience ought to be the brave one.[22]

After the train arrived in New Orleans, Mr. Ben Cason, superintendent of the United States Express Company, Colonel Thomas Boylan, and Post Office Inspector M. A. Fisher interviewed McElroy and Lowrey. The description of the train robber was identical with that of the mysterious Captain Gerald on Carandolet Street, as furnished by Detectives Gaster and Pecora. The police quickly resumed a surveillance of Cora and found that she had ordered three trunks hauled that morning to the railroad depot and the officers reported to Boylan that the baggage was still there at 6 P. M. That evening, full responsibility for investigation of the case was finally given by the express company to Boylan's agency and the detectives were dispatched to the scene on a special train.

Two detectives were immediately assigned, one to watch the trunks at the depot and the other to watch Mrs. Gerald. It was discovered, however, that the police had been incorrect and that her trunks had already gone by the East Louisiana Railroad to Covington at 4 P. M. The other operative, though, located Cora and set up a close observation of her movements. Early Sunday morning, November 4, after borrowing one dollar from her landlady with which to purchase a ticket,[23] she boarded the train for Covington by herself, the detective covertly travelling with her.

At Covington, Cora was met by Pounds who arranged for her and her trunks to be taken by a commercial carrier to the Pounds' home twenty-five miles from town. The detective, an experienced police officer who was well acquainted with this area of Louisiana and was dressed like a typical farmer, began making discreet inquiries around town. He quickly determined that Captain Gerald was none other than Captain E. F. Bunch and that the woman was Cora Ellis of Dallas and not Bunch's wife. He reported this information back to Boylan in New Orleans.

On the next train after that taken by Cora, five or six of Boylan's men rode to Covington. Carrying Winchesters and posing as hunters, the group located horses and went to Pounds' house believing they would find Bunch there. On arrival, the house was thoroughly searched but they could find no trace of him. Pounds denied any knowledge of Bunch's whereabouts, telling the detectives that he had not seen him since October 24.[24]

That evening, after the posse had left, Pounds went out to feed his horse and heard someone call to him from outside the fence. Investigating, he found Bunch who asked him for food. The fleeing outlaw wolfed down what Pounds brought him, then retreated into the nearby woods. During the next two days, Pounds brought him food to his hiding place. Cora frequently visited him in the thicket also. Bunch lied to Pounds that he had only gotten about $4,000 in the robbery, perhaps with a view to defrauding him of a proper share. It was decided that the bonds were worthless as loot.[25] Bunch passed some of the cash over to Cora during his stay, which he had kept wrapped in an oilcloth coat tied with a "shawl strap."

In the meantime, the detectives now believed Bunch was hiding a few miles above Pearlington on Honey Island, which was formed by forks of the Pearl River. Long reputed to be a refuge for outlaws on the dodge, the island was about fifteen miles long and from six to eight miles wide at its center and, since it was subject to frequent flooding, was uninhabited except for wild game. The island, especially at its northern end, was a tangle of cane brakes, and large oak, gum and cypress trees.[26] The island was occasionally visited by hunting parties that would camp in small crude huts built on small hills at the center of the island. Parts of the island were also nothing more than swamp.[27] Boylan's men scoured the area looking for Bunch, well aware of his reputed ability with firearms.

Pounds returned Cora to Covington on Saturday, November 10, so that she could return to New Orleans. On the same day, Postal Inspector Fisher swore out a complaint against Pounds before U. S. Commissioner William Wright in New Orleans for conspiring with Bunch to rob the mails and a warrant for his arrest was issued.[28] With the failure to capture Bunch, the authorities were now concerned that Pounds should be taken into custody before too much more time elapsed and he might possibly also flee. On the afternoon of the 10th, United States Marshal Moorman swore in former Deputy U. S. Marshal John Baker, as well as three of Boylan's agents, Toney, Murphey, and Hebert, and an express company representative, Van

Hook, as deputies. At about four o'clock, they boarded the train and rode to Covington to execute the warrant, arriving at about 8 P. M. The posse had intended to go to Pounds' home to arrest him, but learned that he was in town, although they did not know he had brought Cora to Covington. Armed with shotguns, they arrested him at Henry Smith's grocery store, taking two revolvers from him, as well as the letters purportedly written to him by Bunch from the Indian Territory. When they took their prisoner to the train depot, the posse then discovered Cora's trunks there awaiting shipment to New Orleans. They waited for her to show up, but, when she didn't appear, took Pounds to New Orleans, arriving very early Sunday morning, November 11.[29]

Pounds, dressed in "true backwoodsman style" and wearing a large slouch hat, was taken to the offices of the Farrell and Boylan Detective Agency where the detectives tried to get a statement from him about the robbery. He refused to say anything. Pounds was then taken and placed in the Orleans Parish Prison, but at about 10 A. M., was again taken to the agency where Colonel Boylan and other detectives labored for over an hour to get him to make a statement. Pounds continued to insist that he knew nothing of the train robbery and that Cora had only been a "summer visitor." He stated that she had grown tired of the quiet and that he had taken her to Covington so she could return to New Orleans.

Colonel Boylan fixed a steely glare on Pounds and said, "You are lying, sir; you have not spoken a word of truth, and you know it. We know that you know all about the robbery and the woman's connection with the robbery." Weary of the questioning and confronted by Boylan's determination, Pounds weakened and admitted that he had seen Bunch after the robbery. The absence of a postmark on the purported letter from Bunch had also been hard for Pounds to explain away.[30] He told the detectives everything that he knew about the robbery and Bunch, continuing to insist, however, that he had nothing to do with it. Once his statement was taken, Pounds was returned to the Parish Prison and placed on the third floor to keep him isolated.

In the meantime, the United States Express Company had posted a $1,000 reward for the capture of Bunch,[31] describing him as forty-seven years old, 6'1" tall, of spare build, and weighing about 175 pounds, with long arms. The description said that "his head stoops forward" and that his hair was auburn or brown, but that "any hair on his face will be red unless dyed." Bunch was said to have dark gray eyes, high cheek bones, and an aquiline nose.[32] Telegrams were sent out to various places where Bunch had been know to frequent, including the police in Dallas and Fort Worth and City Marshal Honeycutt in Gainesville.[33]

On Monday morning, November 12, Pounds was taken before U. S. Commissioner Wright and arraigned on the mail tampering charge. Represented by attorney Joseph A. Reid of Amite City, Pounds was remanded to the Parish Prison and a $20,000 bond was set. At the time it was felt that he had enough friends to raise the money.[34]

Boylan's men had maintained a close surveillance of trains coming to New Orleans, waiting to nab Cora Ellis. At 6:30 A. M. on the 12th, she arrived on the Northeastern train with two large Saratoga trunks and carrying a satchel on her arm. The detectives politely took her into custody and she was taken directly to Boylan's office. She was put through an intensive interrogation lasting for five to six hours. The detectives got only "evasive replies" or statements that they knew were not the truth. Cora told them that she had not seen Bunch since October 24, that she knew nothing about the robbery, and that she had gone to Pounds' house merely to spend a few days in the country. When asked how much money she had, she replied that she had $41.11, offering the satchel to them. The detectives opened the satchel and found the amount of money she claimed, as well as a fully-loaded .44-caliber "pug" revolver.

Cora told them that she had borrowed the money from Pounds and that, after he returned her to Covington, she had stayed at the Riggs House there, unaware of Pounds' arrest.

The detectives then advised Cora that she would be searched by a female and that her trunks, which had been sent to police headquarters, would also be searched. She winced, then voluntarily produced from the lining of her dress an additional sixty-five dollars. She was then taken to the Central Police Station where she was thoroughly searched, but no more money was found. Officers of the express company and the railroad were present when the police opened the two large trunks. In one trunk was male and female clothing. Inspecting a woman's velvet jacket, an officer found $200 sewn in the collar. Under relentless questioning, Cora finally broke down and admitted that Bunch had indeed come to Pounds' house after the robbery and given her $1,300, instructing her to return to Texas and to wait there until she heard from him. Begging the officers not to cut up all of her clothes, she pointed out nine articles of clothing in the trunk, including a coat belonging to Bunch, in which money was concealed and the entire $1,300 was soon recovered. Of the total amount of cash taken in the robbery, Bunch had kept about $9,000. The money was identified as having been handled by the express company because of needle holes, resulting from the practice of sewing the envelope in which the currency was contained.

In the second trunk, some of the stolen bonds Bunch had taken were found in a package marked "$25,000." The detectives also found a Smith and Wesson .38-caliber revolver and two small cotton satchels for carrying cartridges, as well as a package of dynamite cartridges rigged with time fuses. It was speculated that Bunch had used one of these to blow the hole in the roof in the earlier train robbery attempt. Also in the trunk were numerous letters to Bunch, as well as several photographs of him. Among the letters was one from Bunch providing a code where symbols were substituted for letters. At the

William W. Howeth of Gainesville, Texas, was a businessman who dealt with Bunch. Howeth became apprehensive after Bunch displayed a pistol at their last meeting. (Courtesy of The Texas Collection, Baylor University.)

bottom of the letter was the notation, "If misunderstood, telegraph or write."[35]

Cora was locked up in the private office of Police Captain Henderson at the Central Police Station, rather than taken to the Parish Prison. A guard was placed on the door by Chief Hennessy with instructions not to admit anyone, even the investigating detectives. Cora refused to eat anything during the day, but finally relented that evening.[36]

Pounds was again questioned by the detectives on Tuesday the 13th, but, on the advice of lawyer Reid, he refused to make any more statements. Cora remained in isolation at the Central Police Station, but the fact that she was being detained without any warrant was beginning to generate some criticism. Chief Hennessy told the newspapers that she was being held as an accessory but, since she was "sick," no affidavit had been made against her so that she would not have to be transferred to the dank and uncomfortable Parish Prison where the care and attention would not be as good. A circular bearing Bunch's photograph was issued and circulated by the detectives.[37]

The news that Bunch was believed to have robbed the Northeastern train produced considerable excitement in his old haunts in Texas. In Gainesville, while former friends were coming to the defense of his reputation as a "moral man," his forgeries were now also coming to light. In Dallas and Fort Worth, he was the major topic of discussion among the sporting society. Several newspapers attempted to connect Bunch with the activities of the Rube Burrow gang. Marshal Cabell told the newspapers he believed that Bunch had been "connected with every train robbery of any note occurring the past few years in Texas."[38] In Gainesville, the local newspaper even went so far as to tell readers that J. Leon Pounds had been identified as the driver in a series of stagecoach holdups committed a year earlier by a "tall, lone highwayman" between San Angelo and Ballinger in Runnels County, leading to the conclusion that Bunch must have been the robber. The source of this startling news was not identified nor was this allegation ever repeated anywhere else.[39]

The detectives searching the Honey Island area finally abandoned the effort on Thursday, November 15, twelve days after the robbery, and returned emptyhanded to New Orleans. They still believed that Bunch was somewhere in the area.[40] Then, on Friday, Cora Ellis mysteriously disappeared from the Central Police Station. Chief Hennessy, remaining tightlipped, refused to comment on where she had gone, saying only that she had been turned over to express company officials, who in turn promptly denied it. The newspapers speculated that the police had gotten all they could from the woman and decided to release her, hoping she might perhaps lead them to Bunch. Cora, however, had boarded a train and returned to her parents' home in Tyler, Texas, although still under surveillance.[41] Her brief part in the life of Eugene Bunch was over.

Pounds had a preliminary examination before U. S. Commissioner Wright on November 24 for conspiracy to rob the United States mails. When the government's attorney announced that two key witnesses could not be located, both sides agreed to an indefinite continuance and Pounds' bond was reduced from $20,000 to $5,000.[42] After a delay in raising the money, the bond was posted on Saturday, December 1, 1888, and Pounds was released to return home,[43] never to stand trial for any part in the crime.

Eugene Bunch had disappeared. Some detectives felt that, having eluded them, he had gone west. One report had him still in New Orleans. Louisiana trains began carrying armed guards and railroad employees were issued Winchester rifles in case Bunch struck again. Other reports had Bunch openly riding the same train he had robbed, as well as freely associating with gambler friends in Amite City in Tangipahoa Parish.[44]

No sooner had the furor over the Northeastern robbery died down when, on December 15, 1888, the Southern Express Company was victimized by two men who robbed the train near

Duck Hill in Northern Mississippi. A conductor and a passenger armed themselves and, in the resulting gunfire, the passenger was shot to death. The two men escaped unharmed.[45] Pinkerton detectives were unable to find a trace of the outlaws and a circular went out describing the suspects. In New Orleans, Superintendent Hennessy studied the description and, in a subsequent conference, declared to Southern Express officials that the leader of the pair was Eugene Bunch.

A series of coincidences led Hennessy to this belief. First Bunch was supposed to have been in Northern Louisiana a few days before the robbery, easily able to travel to Duck Hill. The description provided by witnesses fit him closely: about 36 years old, 170 pounds, 6'1", light complexion, auburn hair, long, drooping moustache, blue eyes, and rawboned and stoop-shouldered. The description of the second man could have resembled Pounds. The detectives focused their attention on Bunch.[46]

In actuality, the robbery had been committed by Rube Burrow and another companion. The confusion over identity allowed Burrow to make a complete escape without detection. Once more, the lives of the two outlaws seemed to be running parallel.

NOTES

1. *New Orleans Daily Picayune*, November 13, 1888.
2. *Bogalusa Daily News*, August 13, 1953.
3. *New Orleans Daily Picayune*, November 13, 1888.
4. *Gainesville* (Texas) *Daily Hesperian*, November 16, 1888.
5. *Daily Hesperian*, August 28, 1892. William Wesley Howeth was born in 1847 in Rusk County, Texas. His family was among the first settlers in Cooke County in 1853, but the next year a tornado killed five members of the family. In 1858, the family went to Southern California, then returned to Texas in 1860, moving to Gainesville in 1868. Howeth married in 1885 and had two children. He was the mayor of Gainesville for two years and died there on August 12, 1913. Johnson, *History of Texans*,

Vol. III, pp. 1531-33.
   6. *Dallas Morning News*, August 25, 1892.
   7. *Dallas Morning News*, August 25, 1892.
   8. *New Orleans Times-Democrat*, August 23, 1892.
   9. *Dallas Daily Times Herald*, August 29, 1888.
   10. *Dallas Morning News*, August 25, 1892. James C. Arnold was born in Georgia in 1851 and came to Texas in 1869. As a young man he worked on a ferry, helped supply beef to railroad contractors, and was in the grocery business. In 1874, he moved to Dallas and was appointed to the police force. One story told after his death was that, in 1878, he faced down notorious gunman Ben Thompson in a saloon and jailed him. He also was part of the many posses in pursuit of train robber Sam Bass across North Texas in 1878. In 1881, he became Deputy Marshal, then was elected City Marshal later in the year. In 1890, his title became Chief of Police and, in 1893, he represented Texas in the organization of the National Chiefs of Police Union. The following year he was the first president of what became the Texas Police Association and served in that office for four years. After an illustrious career as a police officer and progressive police administrator, however, he was accidentally shot during a hunting trip in February, 1898, and died in Dallas a day later. He was so well thought of that he was the first prominent person to lie in state at the Dallas City Hall and his funeral procession was a major event involving a large number of officers from all over Texas.
   11. *St. Tammany Farmer*, November 17, 1888. Some newspaper accounts had Bunch using the alias "Gerard" or "Girard," but this was incorrect.
   12. *New Orleans Times-Democrat*, November 14, 1888.
   13. *New Orleans Daily Picayune*, August 23, 1892.
   14. *Daily Picayune* August 23, 1892.
   15. *Daily Picayune*, November 13, 1888.
   16. *St. Tammany Farmer*, November 17, 1888.
   17. Report of Arrest, M. A. Fisher, U. S. Post Office Department, November 30, 1888.
   18. *New Orleans Daily Picayune*, November 13, 1888.
   19. Report of Arrest, M. A. Fisher.
   20. *New Orleans Daily Picayune*, November 4, 1888; *New Orleans Times-Democrat*, November 4, 1888; *Gainesville* (Texas) *Daily Hesperian*, November 14, 1888; Report of Arrest, M. A. Fisher. Thomas N. Boylan, who was born in New Orleans in 1833, was a detective with the New Orleans police force prior to the Civil War, then served as a detective for the Confederates. After the war he worked as an agent for the Southern Express Company and as a hotel detective. In 1869, New Orleans' banks hired him, Smith Izard, and Michael J. Farrell as detectives for them. In

1874, Boylan was appointed Chief of Police in New Orleans after the unpopular Kellogg government was driven out of office. When President Grant finally caused restoration of the Kellogg administration, Boylan again worked for the banks briefly until reappointed Chief of Police from 1877 until 1882. He resigned and became a partner in a detective agency Farrell had formed in 1880. The agency was a thriving one, having provided security for the 1884 World's Fair. Farrell died in 1885. The agency during Bunch's time had 250 men working for it, all commissioned by the City of New Orleans. *Biographical and Historical Memoirs of Louisiana* (Chicago: The Goodspeed Publishing Company, 1892), Vol. 1, p. 311.

21. *New Orleans Times-Democrat*, March 13, 1893. The United States Express Company asked the Louisiana legislature to pass a bill permitting the Levee Board to issue duplicate bonds and the company supplied an indemnity bond to guarantee the Board against loss in case any of the original bonds turned up. As of March, 1893, fourteen of the bonds had been recovered.

22. *New Orleans Daily Picayune*, November 4, 1888.
23. *St. Tammany Farmer*, November 17, 1888.
24. *St. Tammany Farmer*, November 17, 1888; *New Orleans Daily Picayune*, November 14, 1888.
25. *St. Tammany Farmer*, November 17, 1888.
26. *New Orleans Daily Picayune*, August 23, 1892.
27. *Daily Picayune*, November 13, 1888.
28. Report of Arrest, M. A. Fisher; *St. Tammany Farmer*, November 17, 1888.
29. Report of Arrest, M. A. Fisher; *New Orleans Times-Democrat*, November 12, 1888; *New Orleans Daily Picayune*, November 12, 1888.
30. *New Orleans Times-Democrat*, November 12, 1888; *St. Tammany Farmer*, November 17, 1888.
31. *New Orleans Times-Democrat*, November 10, 1888.
32. *New Orleans Daily Picayune*, August 23, 1892.
33. *Gainesville* (Texas) *Daily Hesperian*, November 14, 1888.
34. *New Orleans Daily Picayune*, November 13, 1888.
35. *New Orleans Times-Democrat*, August 24, 1892; *St. Tammany Farmer*, November 17, 1888.
36. *New Orleans Daily Picayune*, November 13, 1888.
37. *New Orleans Times-Democrat*, November 14, 1888.
38. *New Orleans Daily Picayune*, November 15, 1888.
39. *Gainesville* (Texas) *Daily Hesperian*, November 16, 1888. Although neither Bunch nor Pounds was even remotely involved in the robberies, the story is an interesting one, as gleaned from the *San Angelo* (Texas) *Standard*, October 1, 1887, through June 15, 1889. At about 11:30 P. M. on September 29, 1887, the stagecoach from San Angelo to

Ballinger, approximately thirty miles distant, was held up by a lone bandit on horseback wearing a red bandana over his mouth. He had all of the eight persons on board dismount and put crude bags made from an old slicker over their heads. Perhaps Bunch read about this technique. He then removed over $900 from them. He held them at gunpoint for three hours, waiting for the San Angelo-bound stage from Ballinger. During this time the robber taunted the passengers for being unarmed because of a new Texas law prohibiting the carrying of weapons. Actually, one passenger did have a pistol but later claimed he was afraid it might misfire if he tried to use it. While they waited, one passenger tried to sell the robber a windmill while another asked him to leave him at least enough for a meal. The robber gave him a $20 gold piece, thinking it was a dollar in the darkness, but, upon recounting his loot, later rectified the error. The robber and his prisoners good-naturedly exchanged drinks of whiskey.

When the second stage arrived the robber let the first one go on and held up the second one, following the same procedure as before but only getting $3.35. He was reported as so nervous that one passenger asked him to be more careful with his pistol. The bandit was later described by the two stage drivers, O. Broome and William Ellis, and the passengers as about 5'8" and 135 pounds.

A week later, at about midnight, October 4, a bandit held up the Ballinger-bound stage again at the same place. This time, he only got about three dollars from the five passengers and some contents from the mail sack. The stage coming from Ballinger had taken another road and the robber had to be satisfied with what he had. The homemade hoods the victims had to wear were traced to a slicker purchased recently in San Angelo, but the person buying it could not be identified. After this robbery, the San Angelo and Ballinger Mail and Express Line switched to a daytime-only schedule. The community was highly upset at the brazen crimes.

On October 9, in the nearby town of Coleman, Jim Newsome, a young cowboy already charged with and out on bond for cattle theft, was arrested for the stage robberies. It was alleged that a stage driver and several passengers had identified him, as well as his horse and its gait. He had also been observed spending a considerable amount of money since the robberies. When arraigned before the U. S. Commissioner in Waco, Newsome pleaded his innocence and offered several alibis for his whereabouts when the robberies occurred. In December, after a two-day trial in which he was positively identified as the "lone highwayman," Newsome was sentenced to life imprisonment and sent to a federal penitentiary at Albany, New York. This led to a meeting of citizens in the small towns of Concho and Paint Rock near San Angelo who were convinced of the boy's innocence and passed a resolution to that effect.

The San Angelo community was stunned when, on April 20, 1888, the stage and a hack making a run between the two towns were held up at 10:20 A. M. by a man on foot wearing a slicker and a white bandana over his face. The man's nearby horse was covered with blankets and had sacks over its legs in order to disguise it, but the wind revealed the horse's color to the passengers. After the stage driven by William Ellis was stopped, the driver of the trailing hack, Al Jacks, attempted to turn around but the bandit's pistol convinced him to stop. One passenger threw a gold watch out of the hack and another put forty dollars in his mouth. The twelve persons on the two vehicles placed the crude sacks provided by the bandit over their heads and the robber divested them of two watches and fifty dollars, as well as forty dollars from the mail sack. The bandit joked with his victims and, at the request of one, signed a note: "This is to certify that passengers on the Ballinger and San Angelo Stage Line on April 20th, were no cowards, as they would have fought, if they had had a chance. Rube Burris." The robber had a passenger pass around cigars and freely discussed the previous robbery. A charm taken from one passenger was returned when the robber was told it was a present from the passenger's mother. The victims were held at gunpoint until 3 P. M., waiting for the stage from San Angelo, but the robber finally grew tired and left. Interestingly, had he waited for the other stage, he would have found it occupied by two deputy sheriffs.

    This robbery led to renewed local concern over Newsome's innocence and his attorneys continued to work diligently on his appeal. Driver Ellis, twice victimized, had originally had doubts about Newsome's identity and was now prepared to swear positively that the second man was the same one who had robbed him seven months earlier.

    On June 23, 1888, Al Jacks was driving the stage to Ballinger at about 3 P. M. when a man on foot with a blue silk hankerchief over the lower part of his face stopped the stage at pistolpoint. He made each of the passengers blindfold himself with his own handkerchief and took from them about $260. After about forty-five minutes, the robber generously passed around a flask taken from a passenger, then had Jacks remove one of the horses from the team, mounted it bareback, and rode off. A Runnels County posse with bloodhounds was soon in pursuit, but to no avail. It was determined the next day, as a result of identification by one of the passengers, that the robber was John Gray, known as "Long John," a well-known gambler in the West Texas vicinity. Telegrams were sent out and, on June 28, Gray was arrested in nearby Colorado City.

    Gray was taken to Waco for arraignment and subsequent trial. In the meantime, the San Angelo and Ballinger Stage Line went out of business in August because of the completion of a railroad connecting the two communities.

Gray and seven other prisoners in the McLennan County Jail overpowered a guard on October 8, 1888, and made an escape across the Brazos River. With three others, Gray comandeered a railroad hand car and headed north until a train forced them to abandon the vehicle. Within three hours, however, all escaped prisoners were back in custody.

U. S. Supreme Court Associate Justice L. Q. C. Lamar, on June 14, 1889, reversed the verdict of the trial court and ordered a new trail for Jim Newsome.

40. *New Orleans Daily Picayune*, November 16, 1888.

41. *Daily Picayune*, November 17, 1888; *New Orleans Times-Democrat*, November 17, 1888. It was later stated that, although the $1,300 recovered from Cora Ellis could not be positively identified as that taken in the train robbery, she waived all claims to it in order to secure her release. It was not until August, 1892, that the dynamite fuses were gently dropped in the middle of the Mississippi River by the police from a ferry boat. Cora was later reported to have gone to Galveston, Texas, and opened a millinery shop.

42. *New Orleans Times-Democrat*, November 25, 1888.

43. *Times-Democrat*, December 2, 1888.

44. *Dallas Morning News*, December 13, 1888.

45. Breihan, *Outlaws*, pp. 95-96. Breihan states that Burrow's September 1, 1890, single-handed robbery of the Louisville and Nashville train outside Flomaton, Alabama, was "precedent-shattering" and the first time that such a feat had been pulled off. Obviously, Bunch had already accomplished such a deed. This was Burrow's last train robbery and he was killed on October 8, 1890, in Linden, Alabama, while reportedly trying to escape custody.

46. George W. Agee, *Rube Burrow, King of Outlaws* (Chicago: M. A. Donohue & Co., 1890), pp. 57-59.

6 Escape West

The whereabouts of Eugene Bunch after the Northeastern robbery are unknown. There was considerable speculation, one newspaper alleging that he was thought to have "escaped to the vastnesses of the Rocky Mountains or to some other far away and inaccessible place."[1] The same newspaper, however, also stated that Bunch had been hunted in the swamps and woods of Louisiana, Mississippi, Florida, and Texas, territory with which he was reputed to be quite familiar. It was also considered possible that he left the country and spent his ill-gotten gains while wearing various disguises.[2]

Bunch would later tell a cohort that he had been travelling through Kentucky, Tennessee, Alabama, Georgia, and Mississippi, "doing nothing in particular except moving around." One newspaper reported him in Birmingham, Alabama, drinking and "shooting craps for $10 a throw."[3] A detective on his trail claimed that the outlaw had gone out west after the robbery until about the middle of 1890, then returned to his old haunts in Louisiana, with occasional forays into Georgia, Tennessee, and Kentucky.[4] Another newspaper indicated that, after the robbery, Bunch remained concealed on Honey Island for several weeks, coming out occasionally only for food. Once the search for him was called off, he then supposedly fled to Mexico. Such reports of his whereabouts were so widely conflicting that, whenever law enforcement officials in Louisiana subsequently received information that Bunch had been seen in Washington, Tangipahoa, or St. Tammany Parishes, they usually shrugged their shoulders and passed them off as useless rumors.[5]

A more specific account of his escape was gleaned by one newspaper from other detectives involved in the chase. According to this acount, Bunch stayed on Honey Island about two weeks, then went cross country to Donaldsonville, south of Baton Rouge on the Mississippi River, spending a day there before leaving through the woods with detectives only hours behind him. He turned up a number of days later in El Paso, Texas, where he supposedly took a train for Tombstone, Arizona. Once in Tombstone, Bunch is supposed to have learned somehow that detectives were still in hot pursuit and left for the home of a sister in San Carlos. After several days there, however, a friend allegedly telegraphed a warning and he left immediately.

Bunch supposedly next turned up, according to this version, on the coast of Southern California. When the pursuing detectives arrived several days later, he had already gone into Mexico and was then staying in a hotel at Quaymas. He went from there to Mexico City, then to Monterey, and on to Vera Cruz, where the detectives finally lost all trace of him. The agents were subsequently removed from the investigation by the United States Express Company.[6]

In July of 1889, the Dallas *Morning News* printed a story that Bunch had recently returned to Gainesville disguised as an old man. It was alleged that he registered at the Lindsay House there under the name of John Hinds on June 26, then left on the 28th when a detective arrived in town looking for him. According to the article, area railroad officials had heard that Bunch was in the vicinity and placed guards on their trains. It was even stated that on one of the nights that "Hinds" was in Gainesville, there was an explosion in a building behind the Red River National Bank, which some people believed was set off by Bunch to create confusion while he robbed the bank.[7] This story, apparently given to the *Morning News* by a correspondent in Gainesville, was never mentioned in the daily Gainesville newspaper despite its obvious newsworthiness, if true. As a result, in spite of the specific details, there is little inclination to give the article much credibility.

Beyond these accounts, there is no record of where Eugene Bunch went and what he did in the period from December, 1888, until February, 1892. It's a total blank. He had received widespread notoriety because of his daring exploit and his photograph was in the hands of many law enforcement officials. Physically, he was easy to recognize. Very likely, he stayed on the move, occasionally resorting to disguise, and frequenting dingy saloons and gambling parlors in the smallest towns or losing himself in the anonymous squalor of red light districts in the bigger communities. The money taken in the train robbery helped sustain him for a while. It is also quite conceivable, if not likely, that he was involved in various other crimes during this period.

On May 20, 1889, Flavia Bunch filed a petition for divorce in the 44th District Court of Dallas County, swearing that she had been a resident of the county for at least one year. She alleged that Bunch had abandoned her and their son in March, 1886, and had contributed nothing for her support since then, even though she had been a "kind and true wife" while they were together. Her sister, Minerva, swore that she never saw Bunch mistreat his wife, but that he abandoned her in December, 1885, "of his own free will" and went to Wichita Falls. When the court held a hearing on February 17, 1890, Bunch had been cited by publication but, of course, did not appear. An attorney was appointed to represent his interests and, two days later, Flavia was granted a divorce. She obtained care and custody of fourteen-year old Theodore, although she had to pay for all costs, including twenty-five dollars for her ex-husband's court-appointed attorney.[8] In her petition she made no mention of Bunch's notoriety as a desperado and it can probably be

A drawing adapted from a newspaper illustration of the train robber, Rube Burrow. Bunch was believed by many to have been an aide to Burrow in several robberies. (Courtesy of the Western History Collections, University of Oklahoma.)

safely assumed that she wanted only to get through this distasteful business quickly and resume a quiet life for her and her son out of the unfortunate limelight.

By the spring of 1892, Bunch was back among the familiar haunts of Louisiana and Mississippi. Clearly, he was ready for another train robbery and was scouting out the available opportunities.

Edward Scanlon Hobgood, a short-statured man, known all of his approximately thirty years as "Curnell," was a farmer in Marion County, Mississippi, living near the Pearl River with his wife, Ida or "Shug," and five children.[9] His mother and brother, Rob, lived not very far away, his father having died when he was a small child. He had been partly raised by another Mississippi farmer, Ben J. Duncan, who also lived nearby at the corner of the Pike and Marion Counties, just north of the Washington Parish line.[10] In addition to his domestic side, Curnell Hobgood liked his whiskey, which occasionally produced some meanness. In December, 1891, he was one of a number of witnesses to a fight between two young men in Marion County named Temple and Terrell. Terrell's father, a farmer named Ike Terrell, began to interfere with the combatants when his son started getting the worst of it. Confused shooting broke out between the parties present, including Hobgood. When the smoke cleared, old man Terrell lay dead. Temple was subsequently arrested and convicted of murder.[11]

Sometime in February or March, 1892, Curnell Hobgood and Eugene Bunch came into contact with each other, if not earlier. One account later quoted Hobgood as saying that he received a letter from Bunch to meet him on the Pearl River, which he did, and that Bunch returned home with him.[12] The most frequent accounts, however, quoted the Curnell as saying that he ran into Bunch roaming in the woods near his farm and took him home with him as a guest. The outlaw stayed with the Hobgood family for three or four weeks, regaling them with his exploits as a train robber and being on the dodge. The Curnell and the outlaw became good friends and Bunch proposed that Hobgood join him in robbing a train. Hobgood agreed, although he later claimed it was only on the condition that Bunch do all of the robbing.[13] Bunch was now using the alias of Captain Grice.

The outlaw apparently felt it would take more than two men to rob a train, unlike over three years before. Earlier in the year, railroad and express officials had heard reports that Bunch had been seen in the area again and felt that he might attempt another holdup. A force of men armed with shotguns was placed on most trains, but after some time went by with no attempt at robbery, the guards were withdrawn.[14] There is little doubt that Bunch was aware of the precautions and decided not to take any chance in another single-handed robbery.

Another resident of Marion County was Henry Carneguay, a not-so-bright short, slim man, twenty-one years old. He had a pale face, prominent cheek bones, thin brown hair over a low forehead, and a small thin mustache. One day late in February, 1892, while transporting a load of wood along a road, he met Curnell Hobgood and a tall stranger and casually greeted them. Over the next week or two, he happened to see them again several times, but without anything more than pleasantries exchanged. One day, the stranger, Captain Grice, was introduced to him. Carneguay had already heard local rumors that Grice was really named Bunch. Grice asked him if he wanted to "take a trip with him," indicating he would pay Carneguay well for taking care of his horses. Carneguay did not accept the invitation at first, but, after "Captain Grice" told him that he and the Curnell were going to rob a train, he agreed to go along. The outlaw cautioned him to keep his mouth shut and instructed him to meet them at a small hollow in some woods about a half-mile from the homes of Rob Hobgood and Ben Duncan on the evening of April 13.[15]

Bunch had already tried to recruit another member for this criminal expedition. Late in February or early in March,

Ben Duncan, who had helped raise Curnell Hobgood, approached a neighbor, Will Jones, requesting the address of Jones' cousin, Henry Sherling, indicating that there was someone at Duncan's home who wanted to see him. Sherling had at one time been suspected by people in the area of assisting Bunch in the 1888 Northeastern robbery,[16] although, in fact, he had never met Bunch.

Sherling, who lived near Harriston, Mississippi, had a reputation as a dangerous man, allegedly responsible for the deaths of a number of men in both Louisiana and Mississippi,[17] and was reportedly wanted for murder in Washington Parish. He was described as quick to resent an insult and short-tempered, but never known to rob or steal anything. An official of the Southern Express Company would say of him: "He had killed at least a dozen men and had no more hesitancy in taking a human life than a butcher would in slaughtering a hog, yet he was scrupulously honest and would not steal a cent from anybody."[18] Sherling did not, however, respond to the invitation communicated from Duncan.

Prior to this time, Bunch and Hobgood had cemented their criminal relationship with an outbreak of burglaries and robberies of stores in various small Louisiana towns in the Florida Parishes. A store was robbed at Greensburg, northwest of Amite City. Five days before Mardi Gras, in February, the store of the Babbington Brothers on the Franklinton courthouse square, in Washington Parish, was burglarized. Explosives ripped open the safe and the thieves made off with several hundred dollars. An alert clerk reportedly shot at the fleeing bandits, hitting one of them in the arm. It was later alleged that "Captain Grice" turned up afterwards with his arm in a sling, claiming he had an accident.[19] No one in the area, however, felt compelled to tell the authorities of his suspicions.

At about 7 P. M. on Wednesday, April 13, 1892, as directed, Henry Carneguay met with Curnell Hobgood and Bunch in the hollow. The three mounted their horses and rode southwest, crossing into Louisiana. Travelling all night, they maintained silence most of the way and took care not to be seen. They ate a quick cold meal from their saddlebags along the way. Toward the end of the trip, in Tangipahoa Parish, Bunch discussed the robbery with his two companions. At daybreak, they stopped and pitched their horses in a thicket, then moved them to the edge of a field about a mile or two from the Illinois Central Railroad track. The sound of a passing train could be clearly heard.

Bunch told his companions that he was going to either Arcola or south to Hammond and ride back on the train, indicating he wanted Hobgood to meet him at the track, about one-half mile south of Amite City, not far from Newsom's Mill. Carneguay was left to watch the horses as Bunch and Hobgood walked off, Bunch probably relating the details of his plan to the Curnell. Bunch then set off alone on foot, walking all day approximately eighteen miles south to Hammond.

Left to wait, the two men shared another cold meal, staying with the horses until the sun began to set. Hobgood then had Carneguay come with him to the track about an hour before they expected the train. Hobgood carried a rifle and Carneguay had Bunch's rifle, which he gave to Hobgood. The Curnell gave him a small pistol which Carneguay put in his pocket. Hobgood instructed him to shoot if anyone attempted to interfere with him during the robbery.[20]

Passenger Train Number Two of the Illinois Central Railroad, northbound from New Orleans, made its usual stop at Hammond around 8 P. M., brightly illuminated by the lunch pavillion at the station. A little further up the track, however, the engine was in the shadows. As Engineer C. C. Jarvis and the fireman began to move the train out of the station, a poorly-dressed man wearing a white slouch hat, gray pants torn and tattered at the bottom, and a dirty yellow slicker, appeared in the cab with them. The tall man wore a cheap pair of lapped buckle brogan shoes and had a mask over the lower part of his face, although it was obvious he had a full beard.

The intruder thrust a revolver at them and ordered them to "go right on and do what I tell you and there will be no trouble." He instructed them to "run along lively and stop at the seventy-seven mile post," asking the engineer if he knew where that was. When Jarvis replied that he wasn't sure, the masked man gave him directions to stop about 300 yards past the second trestle the train crossed. The fire box was low and the bandit allowed them to feed it more coal. Loading the coal, the open fire box illuminated the cab, giving both men an opportunity to get a good look at their uninvited guest.

Over the noise of the locomotive, Jarvis told the bandit that they would be meeting southbound Passenger Train Number Three at Independence, between Hammond and Amite City, and would have to temporarily pull off and stop on a siding. A flagman there would open and close the switch. The tall man told them, "That's all right; but don't you let anybody get on this engine and don't you make any signs to anybody that would in any way announce my presence; for if you do, I'll kill you!" When the train stopped on the siding, the other train thundering by for New Orleans, the flagman attempted to get on the engine as was his custom, but the engineer headed him off without any explanation. The train then resumed its journey north.

As the train approached the 77-mile post south of Amite City at about 8:30 P. M., the bandit ordered it stopped. Seeing the train coming, Carneguay took a post on the west side of the track, the Curnell on the east. When the train was fully stopped, the three shabbily-dressed bandits escorted the engineer and the fireman back to the express car, the fireman directed to bring the axe from the tender car. Jarvis and the fireman were instructed to knock and tell the Southern Express messenger, George Matthews, to open up. Just at this time, Conductor W.

S. Robinson and other members of the train crew approached them in the darkness to see why the train had stopped. Jarvis, at the direction of Bunch, called out to them: "Look out! We're in the hands of train robbers. They'll kill you." Inside the car, Express Messenger Matthews heard the warning, hurriedly locked the safe, and began hiding valuables behind freight boxes, in the stove, and in his own pockets. He then fled the express car to cars in the rear of the train, shedding his overalls and cap as he went. He hid in the rear sleeper car.

When the express car was not opened up on demand, the robbers forced a door open on the west side of the car and entered. Irritated at this delay, one of the trio struck the baggageman on the side of the head with a revolver, accusing him of being the express messenger and of trying to thwart them. The frightened man swore that he was only the baggagemaster and pleaded for his life. One of the bandits, probably Bunch, attacked the small safe with the fireman's axe, his mask slipping off from the movement and exertion. Finally, the safe was opened and the contents were quickly removed. Jarvis was told to cover the train headlight and back the train about 200 yards, then go ahead and resume the northward trip. In this way, the train crew would have difficulty seeing their direction or means of flight in the darkness. The bandits made no attempt to enter the mail car or to disturb any of the passengers.[21]

When the train backed up, the outlaws climbed over a fence and ran back to where their horses were tied by the field. They rode quickly from the scene, Bunch carrying a sack containing the booty from the train. About six miles away, they stopped to inspect their haul. It was disappointing. There was only about $500 in cash, the remainder being worthless New York drafts and Louisiana lottery tickets. There were also three packages of jewelry, including medals for a school exhibition.[22] The disgusted bandits moved on, stopping again about an hour before sunrise. A fire was built and Bunch burned the useless drafts and lottery tickets. Carneguay was given a silver-cased watch as his part of the loot and promised some money later. Bunch gave Hobgood $100, then the three separated.[23]

After leaving Newsom's Mill at the 77-mile post, Engineer Jarvis sped the train to Tangipahoa several miles north, rather than Amite City, and telegraphed J. W. Higgins, the trainmaster at McComb City, Mississippi, of the robbery. Higgins promptly telegraphed the railroad's headquarters in New Orleans at about 9:35 P. M. and Superintendent Dunn rushed over from his hotel to learn the particulars. Higgins also notified Sheriff Mix at Amite City and a deputy at Tangipahoa. Sheriff Webb of Jackson, Mississippi, was contacted about the possibility of bloodhounds being brought from the Mississippi State Penitentiary on a special train to help in the search for the robbers. Sheriff Mix was requested not to allow the members of his posse to do anything that might destroy the scent.[24]

In Jackson, Mississippi, Southern Express detective Thomas V. Jackson was also notified of the robbery and he accompanied the bloodhounds on the train, arriving at Newsom's Mill at about 3 A. M. the next morning. However, the bloodhounds were not able to pick up a scent and had to be returned. It also turned out that Sheriff Mix had not organized a posse or conducted a search. As one newspaper reported: "There is very little excitement over the matter here, as the people do not care to risk their lives in attempting to capture the outlaws unless a sufficient reward is offered to induce them to do so."[25] Joining Detective Jackson at the scene were Southern Express Superintendent H. C. Fisher and another express company detective, M. J. O'Brien, who, like Jackson, had played a role in the chase after Rube Burrow over a year-and-a-half earlier.

In New Orleans, former detective and now chief of police Gaster declared: "If the notorious Captain Bunch was not with them, the trio were his pupils."[26] In an editorial, the *Daily Picayune* repeated its familiar lament that train robbery was far too successful and that so long as it remained an enterprise rela-

Edward Scanlon Hobgood, the "Curnell," helped Bunch rob the Illinois Central and was with him at his death. (Courtesy of Mrs. Audrey Johnson.)

tively free of risk, more such robberies would be encouraged. "A little boldness and the necessary pistols are all the stock in trade required by the robbers, and the business, besides being profitable, commends itself by its dash and daring to the romantic young rascals who in an earlier generation would have run away to the west to shoot indians and buffaloes."[27]

On April 16, the Southern Express Company offered a $1,000 reward for the arrest and conviction of the train robbers. Everyone was quite aware that the description of one of the bandits tallied exactly with that given of Eugene Bunch in 1888. But, after April 17, newspaper accounts of the robbery and the subsequent efforts to track down the culprits disappeared from the newspapers. The crime was relegated to a lesser priority as a common topic of public conversation. It appeared that, as more time passed, the trail of the robbers had grown cold and, as in so many other robberies, they likely would not be apprehended.

NOTES

1. *New Orleans Times-Democrat*, August 19, 1892.
2. *Times-Democrat*, August 23, 1892.
3. *Times-Democrat*, August 23, 1892; *New Orleans Delta*, August 23, 1892 (quoted in Magee, *Eugene Bunch Story*, pp. 32-41); *Birmingham* (Alabama) *Age-Herald*, March 4, 1889 (quoted in William Stanley Hoole, *The Saga of Rube Burrow*, University, Alabama: Confederate Publishing Co., 1981, p. 61).
4. *New Orleans Times-Democrat*, August 23, 1892.
5. *New Orleans Daily Picayune*, August 23, 1892.
6. *Daily Picayune*, August 23, 1892.
7. *Dallas Morning News*, July 10, 1889.
8. Petition, 44th District Court, Dallas County, Texas, cause no. 7431, May 30, 1889; Minutes, 44th District Court, Dallas County, Texas, cause no. 7431, Vol. 1, p. 293.
9. Interviews by author with Thomas V. Hobgood (August 13, 1981) and Mrs. Rastus Hobgood (August 8, 1981). The spelling of Curnell comes from a family Bible.

10. This area has since been included in Walthall County.

11. *New Orleans Times-Democrat*, August 24, 1892.

12. *New Orleans Delta*, August 23, 1892 (quoted in Magee, *Eugene Bunch Story*, pp. 32-41).

13. *New Orleans Times-Democrat*, August 23, 1892; *New Orleans Daily Picayune*, August 23, 1892.

14. *New Orleans Daily Picayune*, April 16, 1892.

15. *Daily Picayune*, August 19, 1892; *New Orleans Times-Democrat*, August 19, 1892.

16. *New Orleans Times-Democrat*, August 23, 1892.

17. *Times-Democrat*, August 12, 1892.

18. *New Orleans Picayune*, August 14, 1892.

19. *Daily Picayune*, August 14, 23, 1892.

20. *Daily Picayune*, August 19, 1892; *New Orleans Times-Democrat*, August 19, 1892.

21. *New Orleans Daily Picayune*, April 15-17, 1892, August 19, 1892; *New Orleans Times-Democrat*, April 15-17, 1892, August 19, 23, 1892.

22. *New Orleans Daily Picayune*, April 15-17, 1892; *New Orleans Times-Democrat*, April 15-16, 1892.

23. *New Orleans Times-Democrat*, August 19, 23, 1892; *New Orleans Daily Picayune*, August 19, 1892.

24. *New Orleans Times-Democrat*, April 15, 1892.

25. *Times-Democrat*, April 16, 1892.

26. *New Orleans Daily Picayune*, April 16, 1892. New Orleans Police Chief David Hennessy had been assassinated by what many alleged were members of the Mafia. Subsequently, a mob stormed the Parish Prison and lynched a number of suspects.

27. *Daily Picayune*, April 16, 1892.

7 In Pursuit of Bunch

Feeling more secure, Bunch and Hobgood returned to the familiar Louisiana-Mississippi border locale. The area had come to be considered a dangerous area locally because of their escapades and it was stated that the inhabitants of the countryside lived in constant terror. Hobgood, who had now abandoned steady farming, was said to have drunkenly galloped his horse around a churchyard, using trees for target practice and defying anyone to try to claim the reward for him. He declared that he would not be taken alive.[1] While it was alleged that the residents of the area were friendly to Bunch and were quick to assist him in hiding from the law, Hobgood himself would later say that it was "more through fear than otherwise."[2]

Henry Carneguay, on the other hand, was not feeling so secure. He heard nothing more from his fellow desperadoes and grew increasingly frightened of capture. He kept his share of the loot, the silver watch, carefully out of sight. Finally, about three or four weeks after the robbery, he nervously threw the watch into the furnace at the mill where he worked for Rob Hobgood, the Curnell's brother.[3]

In the meantime, the detectives were still working diligently to find a trace of the trio. Tom Jackson enjoyed a widespread reputation as a competent detective, having successfully solved a number of cases for the Southern Express Company in the Southeastern states. Just under six feet tall, about forty years old, and with a neat brown moustache, the stocky detective was a jovial man who enjoyed his cigars. He had been reared in Monroe County, Mississippi, and went west for several years as a young man. He returned and settled at Aberdeen, Mississippi, beginning his career as a detective for Southern Express.[4]

Jackson's reputation was largely derived from his involvement in the pursuit of Rube Burrow. Pinkerton and express company detectives had doggedly pursued Burrow and his gang, but had been continually frustrated in each attempt to lay a trap. When Burrow cold-bloodedly murdered a postmaster in Lamar County, Alabama, in June of 1889, the manhunt intensified. Jackson arrested a cousin of Burrow, leading to important information on Burrow's criminal activities. Jackson then participated in the manhunt that ultimately led to Burrow's capture and subsequent death.[5]

Another Southern Express detective who joined Jackson in the search for the train robbers was Charles O. Summers. Standing about 5'9" tall, he wore a blond moustache and was just as fond of a good cigar as Jackson. Summers had formerly been a yardmaster in Chicago for the Illinois Central Railroad. In 1889, while in Chicago, he was cited as a hero for snatching a baby from its carriage, which was on the railroad tracks, and falling back with the baby onto the cowcatcher of a train an instant before it smashed into the carriage. Summers moved to New Orleans where he also worked as yardmaster for the Illinois Central.

Believing himself to be a talented pugilist, Summers quit the railroad and went into training. He was scheduled to meet a prominent professional boxer, Tommy Danforth, at the Audubon Athletic Club in New Orleans. Danforth whipped him soundly and the loss was kindly blamed on overtraining and lack of experience. Summers then dropped out of sight briefly, emerging as a Southern Express detective. Initially, Jackson assigned him to watch the trains in Meridian, Mississippi, while posing as an express company solicitor,[6] but then called him to New Orleans.

Jackson had scoured the area of the train robbery for over a week after the robbery and found that the bandits had crossed the Tangipahoa River approximately two miles east of the 77-mile point. He located a local Negro man who had seen three men before the robbery and who was able to describe their horses. Ultimately, Jackson was able to backtrack them through Washington Parish. One of the horses used by the robbers matched the description of a horse known to belong to Curnell Hobgood. Jackson also heard about "Captain Grice" and easily deduced that it was none other than Eugene Bunch.

The detective knew how dangerous Bunch and Hobgood were and that it would be foolhardy to venture alone into their country. During his investigation in Washington and Tangipahoa Parishes, he heard about Henry Sherling and the gossip that had connected him with Bunch in both the 1888 Northeastern robbery and now this crime. Checking out the lead, Jackson went to Jefferson County, north on the Mississippi River, and, checking among neighbors, satisfied himself that Sherling had not been involved in the recent train robbery with Bunch, although Sherling was acquainted with Hobgood and Ben Duncan. Taking a direct approach, the detective went to Sherling, ate dinner with him, and frankly explained that he was trying to track down the train robbers. After dinner, strolling in a field, Sherling told Jackson that he had received a letter from his cousin, Will Jones, that he was a suspect in the offense. He explained his fear that Jackson was there to arrest him for the robbery and that, if need be, he was ready to go. The detective assured him that he was satisfied that Sherling had no part in the robbery but that, because of his reputation as a bad man and his many contacts, he wanted Sherling's assistance in capturing the robbers. Although he did not reveal who he suspected, Jackson was careful to also mention the possibility of Sherling receiving part of the $1,000 reward being offered. Sherling hesitated,

Eugene F. Bunch posed for this photograph sometime in the 1880's and it was used for his wanted poster. (Courtesy of Ed Bartholomew.)

considering the need to attend to his farm as well as the robbery. However, he relented and agreed to help.⁷

When Jackson theorized as to who he suspected were the culprits, Sherling agreed with the conclusion. He told the detective about the previous contact that Ben Duncan had attempted to make with him through Will Jones several months before. Jackson quickly saw the opportunity to use Jones' letter as a foot in the door and instructed Sherling to go to Duncan's residence. Sherling was to show Duncan the letter and explain that he delayed in responding because he was afraid that Duncan was trying to lure him into a trap to arrest him for murder.

After working out the details of how he would stay in contact with Jackson, Sherling travelled to see Ben Duncan in Marion County. The old farmer told him that the Curnell and "Grice" had wanted him to join them in the April train robbery. Sherling expressed his regrets at having missed the opportunity and spent the night at Duncan's house. The next morning, he went to Hobgood's place where the two greeted each other warmly. Hobgood was nervous about reports of detectives roaming through the woods looking for him. Riding around that day to see if they could actually spot some detectives, Sherling casually tried to get the Curnell to talk about the train robbery, but Hobgood would say nothing. They spent the night at Duncan's place and the next day Hobgood finally told him about the train robbery.

Hobgood told Sherling that they had sent a letter to him in the name of Simmons at Harriston, Mississippi, inviting him to join them. Sherling had not received the letter. The Curnell complained that the robbery had been nothing but a "water haul." He gave Sherling a watch and chain from the robbery and asked him to try and sell it in Mississippi, indicating that thirty-five dollars would be a good price for it.

On the subject of Bunch, Hobgood said that he still preferred the "Grice" alias and that he was "on a trip." He was expected to return in about eight days and, when he did, the two of them would then come to Sherling's farm, probably within two weeks.

Sherling stayed with the Curnell a day or two longer, then met secretly with Jackson at a pre-arranged time and location near Tangipahoa. He gave the detective the watch and carefully related all of the details of this initial meeting. Sherling then returned to his Mississippi farm and waited. When the outlaws did not show up at the end of the two weeks, Jackson advised him to wait two or three days longer. No doubt, a squad of detectives was in place and poised to nab the two bandits. Still, they did not come. As directed, Sherling then wrote Hobgood that he had sold the watch and asked if he should send the money or wait for them. Four or five days later, a letter arrived from Hobgood asking him to bring the money to him. Jackson gave him the thirty-five dollars to give Hobgood.

Sherling rode down to Hobgood's place where the Curnell told him that he had heard nothing from "Grice" but was expecting him at any time. The two stayed together for about a week in the area but Bunch still did not appear. Sherling told the Curnell that he would have to return home to see about his crops, but he was urged to stay as "Grice" should be there soon and was anxious to meet with him. Several days later, even though the missing outlaw still had not shown up, Hobgood proposed the robbery of a rich old farmer named Lingland who lived about fifteen miles from his place. He explained that he would write to "Grice" and have him join them near Lingland's farm on the night planned for the holdup.[8]

Again secretly meeting Jackson near Tangipahoa, Sherling expressed his reservations about participating in the robbery. Jackson astutely recognized that Bunch and Hobgood were still not sure of Sherling and were going to use this robbery as a test of his loyalty. He told Sherling that he should go along with the robbery and accept his share of the loot. Jackson promised that the detectives would try to trap them as soon as possible and return everything that was taken to the farmer. Agreeing to this,

Sherling left and returned to Hobgood's home.

On the night scheduled for the robbery, Hobgood and Sherling waited near the farmer's home, but Bunch did not make an appearance, his absence later blamed on high water. Hobgood suggested that the two of them go ahead and pull the robbery themselves. However, when they neared Lingland's farm, they discovered he had visitors and decided to hold off for several days. Two days later, Dave Carr, a neighbor, came by Hobgood's place and told them about general gossip in the community to the effect that the two of them were working with Bunch and that folks anticipated there would be a robbery somewhere soon. This news led Hobgood to abandon the plan to rob the farmer, apparently not wanting to attract any more police attention.

Sherling told Hobgood that he was tired of all of this and was going to quit and go home. Obviously, Bunch had no intention of showing up. Hobgood told him that Bunch could not afford to "go back on them" and proposed waiting for two more weeks. If the absent Captain Bunch did not come by then, the two of them would "leave the country" together. Sherling agreed to go along with this idea.

On the way to another meeting with Jackson on Friday, August 5, 1892, Sherling ran into an acquaintance of his and Hobgood's, Huey Magee. Magee told him that there was a rumor that Sherling was there to trap the Curnell for the Terrell murder in Mississippi and get the reward. During their many conversations, Hobgood had boasted to Sherling that it was quite funny that another person should be in prison for a crime that he had committed. "Huey, you know me too well for that," Sherling replied calmly. Magee agreed that Sherling would never give Hobgood away, but the rumor was a strong one.

Sherling immediately passed this information on to Jackson, although he was convinced that Hobgood did not suspect him at all. Jackson told him to return to Hobgood's, rather than back to his own farm as he had told Hobgood he would. The detective proposed that Sherling tell the Curnell in a joking manner what Magee had said and, in so doing, allay any suspicions the rumors might have created. Jackson also told him to stay with Hobgood until the evening of Thursday, August 11, when the detective would meet him again at Monroe McElveen's place in Washington Parish. After the meeting, Jackson returned to New Orleans.[9]

During this time, the detectives had developed a number of schemes to capture Bunch and his cohorts. One elaborate scheme later reported involved Sherling maneuvering Bunch and Hobgood into trying another train robbery. A decoy train containing a squad of heavily armed men would lure them to a designated site and the posse would attempt, if possible, to capture the bandits alive. Eight men were selected for the task and were provided with new Winchester rifles, pistols, and ammunition purchased from a New Orleans hardware store. Seven of the posse were recruited from the Mississippi cities of Jackson and Aberdeen. An eighth man from Summit, Mississippi, who had volunteered in 1888 to track down Bunch but had been refused, was also selected. When Bunch was subsequently not captured in 1888, he had accused the detectives of not wanting to capture the outlaw. The posse boarded the decoy train, the plan having been carefully coordinated with Sherling. However, the train passed through the designated holdup point without incident. It was later learned from Sherling that a violent rainstorm had prevented the bandits, supposedly including Bunch, from getting to the railroad.[10]

There was ample reason to be concerned about the secrecy of Sherling's mission, especially because of the prevailing rumors about him wanting to betray Hobgood. Some detectives felt that Bunch had spies, even in New Orleans, monitoring every move they made. No doubt, the longer the charade was carried on, the harder it would be to maintain secrecy. One obstacle to the security of the operation, unfortunately, was Sherling himself. He had confided his activities to his lawyer in Amite City, Joe Reid. Reid later stated that he was approached by Lucious Lampton of Tylertown, Mississippi, who told him that Sherling was suspected of being involved in an earlier robbery of Lampton's store. The suspicion was strong enough, according to Reid, that he feared Sherling would be lynched shortly. To head off such a killing, Reid revealed Sherling's undercover role, confident, of course, that Lampton would never leak the information. Reid, who later claimed that he had been accused of revealing Sherling's activities, asserted that it was common knowledge that Sherling was acquainted with Detective Jackson and that the two had been seen together. He stated that some Negro men who worked for Monroe McElveen, where the two frequently met, had inadvertently told Curnell Hobgood about them meeting there.[11] Obviously, if Sherling was foolishly telling his friends of his covert activities, it would not remain a secret for long.

On Sunday, August 7, two days after Sherling met with Jackson, he and Hobgood went to Ben Duncan's place in Marion County. Possibly, there was some reason for Sherling to believe that the evasive Bunch was finally going to meet with them and lay some plans for a new criminal venture. Duncan gathered up his family that morning and went to church thirteen miles away, one newspaper later alleging that this was the first time in eighteen months that they had gone to church. Left alone, Sherling and Hobgood ate some watermelon. At about noon, the Curnell left the house to get his horse which was tied a short distance away. Sherling followed him, walking out of the house and stepping off the porch. A rifle shot shattered the stillness and a .45-caliber slug slammed into Sherling's left arm and travelled upwards, exploding his face. He was dead before he hit the ground.

When he heard the shot, Hobgood whirled and saw Sherling fall. Thinking it was a posse after him, he panicked and, clutching his rifle, ran down a dirt road to Bob Duncan's place, three-quarters of a mile away. Duncan, who was Ben Duncan's

Ida Magee Sherling, after her husband was murdered by Bunch, was moved with her children to New Orleans by the Illinois Central Railroad. (Courtesy of Mrs. Zuma F. Magee.)

brother, heard the shot and several minutes later saw Hobgood run breathlessly up to his place. The Curnell gasped that Sherling had been shot and that "they" were after him, then resumed running in the August heat. He stopped again about a mile down the road at the Payne place where he repeated the story.

Eugene Bunch had heard the rumors circulating about Henry Sherling. Wary, he had been careful to avoid falling into any trap that the detectives might try to set for him. Gradually, the pieces began to fall into place and there was little doubt in the outlaw's mind that Sherling was working for the detectives. Knowing, apparently through some communication with either Hobgood or Ben Duncan, that Sherling would be at Duncan's home on Sunday, perhaps even setting the meeting up himself, the outlaw methodically planned the informer's death. He cleared a position in some thick weeds just beyond a rail fence about 100 feet from the house, giving him a clear view of the front of the house. When Sherling stepped off the porch, Bunch calmly shot him with his .45-caliber Winchester, then left while Hobgood raced down the road.[1 2]

When news of Sherling's death was first made public, it was quickly assumed that either Bunch or Hobgood had killed him. The Duncan family's trip to church was seen as a convenient alibi for an assassination that had been carefully planned. Duncan himself was then believed to have been involved in the April train robbery as the third person. Sherling's role as an agent of the detectives was revealed and his death forged a renewed commitment by the detectives to run down the outlaws.

The next day, August 8, Charles Summers gathered up camera equipment and a few copies of the *Police Gazette* and went to Amite City. Posing as a *Gazette* reporter who had been covering a prizefight in New Orleans and who wanted to do a story on the Sherling killing, he asked around the small town for information. Not finding much, he rode horseback some forty miles to Ben Duncan's farm across the state line. He told

Duncan that he wanted a sketch of the house for the story and Duncan obliged by showing the detective around, pointing out the spot where Sherling had fallen. The detective explored the vicinity, according to a later interview, and found the spot Bunch had cleared out to wait for Sherling to come out of the house. He also interviewed Bob Duncan and other people in the area, satisfying himself that Hobgood probably had nothing to do with the murder, given his obvious panic and spontaneous flight when Sherling went down. Summers also claimed later that he found a .45-caliber cartridge shell at the ambush site in the weeds where Bunch had waited. Bunch was the only person in that area known to have a .45-caliber Winchester rifle.[13]

Tom Jackson, unaware of what had occurred, returned to Amite City from Mississippi on Thursday, August 11, to keep his scheduled appointment with Sherling at Monroe McElveen's. When he learned of the murder, he decided that the time had come to "select a posse of reliable men and go through that country in search of Sherling's slayers, with the intention of remaining there till I ran them out, killed them, or captured them."[14]

Returning to New Orleans, Jackson and Summers huddled together, laying plans for the expedition. Telegrams were sent to men Jackson knew well and could rely on: John Jackson and Dave Martin of Aberdeen, Mississippi, and Jack Kane, Pete Baxter, and Horace Perry of Jackson, Mississippi. The men were notified to be in Osyka, a small town in Mississippi's Pike County just above the Louisiana border about twenty miles north of Amite City. The rifles, pistols and ammunition bought for the aborted decoy train were boxed and sent from New Orleans to Osyka for use by the posse.

On Sunday morning, August 14, as scheduled, the men assembled in the small town, discussed their plan, and mounted their horses. Grimly determined, the posse set out to once and for all end the criminal career of Eugene Bunch.

NOTES

1. *New Orleans Times-Democrat*, August 18, 1892.
2. *Times-Democrat*, August 23, 1892.
3. *Times-Democrat*, August 19, 1892.
4. *Times-Democrat*, August 23, 1892; *New Orleans Delta*, August 23, 1892 (quoted in Magee, *Eugene Bunch Story*, pp. 32-41).
5. Breihan, *Outlaws*, pp. 96-101.
6. *New Orleans Times-Democrat*, August 23, 1892, December 12, 13, 1892. Some newspaper accounts referred to Summers as a Pinkerton detective, but there is no indication that this was correct. William Pinkerton inferred fifteen years later that his agency "acted with a special officer of the Southern Express Company and a local official" in the pursuit of Bunch. Pinkerton, *Train Robberies*, p. 51.
7. Another account of Sherling's involvement in the Bunch investigation attributed his recruitment to the personal efforts of Southern Express Company Superintendent H. C. Fisher, rather than T. V. Jackson. Most of the description of Sherling's activities in this chapter were drawn from an interview with Jackson. The specificity of his comments in that interview, plus the fact that his statements were never refuted, force the conclusion that the detective alone worked with Sherling, although he most certainly kept his superiors advised of the investigation's progress.
8. Another newspaper account identified the robbery scheme as directed at a store owned by a man named Singleton and that the robbery was actually carried off, Jackson returning the amount stolen to the storeowner. It is highly unlikely that this occurred, though.
9. *New Orleans Times-Democrat*, August 23, 1892.
10. *New Orleans Daily Picayune*, August 23, 1892.
11. *New Orleans Times-Democrat*, August 24, 1892. Considering later events, it is not likely that Hobgood learned of the meetings with the detective, or, if he did, there is no information to indicate that he intended to act on that information.
12. *Times-Democrat*, August 12, 23, 1892; *New Orleans Daily Picayune*, August 10, 14, 1892. In the Hobgood family the story has been passed down that Sherling was killed as he was putting remnants of the watermelon in a hog trough and that his body was moved much later after the hogs had feasted on the gore. (Interview with Mrs. Rastus Hobgood, August 8, 1981). Today Henry Sherling lies in an unmarked grave on a farm several miles southwest of Franklinton. After his death, the Illinois Central Railroad moved his wife and children to New Orleans and provided jobs for all of them.

13. *New Orleans Times-Democrat*, August 23, 1892. In a letter to the editor of the *Times-Democrat* on August 24, lawyer Joe Reid, in addition to denying that it was he who gave Sherling away, claimed that the .45-caliber cartridge shell was sent to him by Will Jones and that he gave that shell to Summers in Amite City. Perhaps Summers was merely embellishing his personal role in the investigation, as he and Jackson were basking in considerable newspaper attention. Others would later question Summers' conclusions in clearing Hobgood of any role in Sherling's death.

14. *Times-Democrat*, August 23, 1892.

Southern Express Detective Thomas V. Jackson tracked down Rube Burrow and Eugene Bunch. (Courtesy of Mississippi Department of Archives and History.)

8 The End of Bunch

Leaving Osyka on the morning of August 14, the posse rode steadily southeast, reaching Franklinton that evening. They rested their horses there and recruited five local men to assist in the manhunt: Warren Magee, W. J. Jones, Clay Campbell, W. Y. Wood, and J. B. Caldwell. At about 10 P. M. that same evening, the posse started out again, riding north about twenty miles to Ben Duncan's farm across the state line. They arrived there about 5 A. M. Monday morning and promptly arrested the grey-bearded Duncan. The posse then immediately went to Curnell Hobgood's house to also take him into custody, but he wasn't there. After a brief search of the area around the house, Jackson concluded that the Curnell had probably taken to the swamps and the posse returned to Ben Duncan's place.[1]

Under intensive interrogation, Duncan finally admitted harboring Bunch and Hobgood, both before and after the train robbery. He had even given the outlaws a sack of corn with which to feed their horses when they left to meet the train. He told the detectives, however, that he had been afraid that if he refused to feed and conceal them, they would have killed him. He also revealed for the first time that Henry Carneguay was the third member of the bandit team. At their insistent urging, Duncan agreed to help the posse in its search.[2]

Even though both men and horses were exhausted from the all-night ride and the attempt to locate Hobgood, the posse did not want to waste any time. With Duncan accompanying them, the men entered the swamps just north of Duncan's house. Recent heavy rains had made the roads difficult to use. After about three hours of aimless looking around in the swamps, the posse came across a Negro man who told them that Henry Carneguay worked for Rob Hobgood.

The posse headed for Rob Hobgood's house. When they arrived, they acted as if they were looking for the Curnell. No mention was made of Carneguay so as not to frighten him off. The Hobgood house was searched by Jackson for any photographs of the Curnell while Summers interviewed Hobgood's mother. Through indirect questioning, he learned that Carneguay had gone to a neighbor's house about three miles away to get a yoke of oxen. Jackson and Summers, with Duncan and two other men, set out to intercept Carneguay on his return, the rest of the posse staying behind to guard the house.

After riding a short distance, the posse spotted a young man wearing a white shirt and a straw hat with some oxen and concluded that it was Carneguay. They rode up to him and pointed their rifles menacingly, ordering him to throw up his hands. Terrified, Carneguay did as he was told, but a member of the posse, probably nervous as well as exhausted, fired a shot that whistled by Carneguay's head into the woods. Without saying a word, Jackson and Summers dismounted and brought a rope with a noose over to the bandit. The noose was put around his neck and drawn taut, then Carneguay was shuffled to a nearby tree. Going through the motions of preparing for a lynching, Jackson finally broke the silence and asked him about his part in the train robbery. In spite of his fear and the belief that he was about to die, Carneguay strongly denied any involvement.

A member of the posse struck Carneguay vigorously in the stomach with the butt of a rifle. Yielding to his terror, he confessed to the robbery, exonerating Ben Duncan of any active role in the crime, although the detectives did not believe that. Carneguay told them that he had seen the Curnell several times since he had burned the silver watch, but he had no idea where he or Bunch were now. He claimed that he had been "led into" the robbery by Bunch and Hobgood and did not understand what he was doing. All he did, he said, was to stand outside the train while the other two committed the robbery.

Taking Carneguay into custody, the posse returned to Duncan's house. That evening, the two prisoners were taken to Franklinton. It had been a long, hard day and Jackson decided to let both men and horses rest for a day before resuming the manhunt. Duncan and Carneguay were placed in the Washington Parish Prison.

On Thursday morning, August 18, the refreshed men rode west to Amite City and took Carneguay before District Judge Robert R. Reid. District Attorney Bolivar Edwards had filed a bill of information against the young bandit and he plead guilty to robbery before the judge. When asked if he knew the consequences of his plea, Carneguay said, "I am guilty and am here at your mercy, being forced to do what I did." Judge Reid sentenced him to five years at hard labor in the State Penitentiary. While this was happening, posse members Perry, Kane, and Baxter left the chase and returned to Jackson, Mississippi. Carneguay was handcuffed, shackled, and placed on a train and taken to New Orleans, where he was lodged in the Central Police Station.[3] Elated by their success, the remaining members of the posse were wagering that they would have Bunch and Hobgood in their grasp within two days.

Continuing newspaper reports of the manhunt had stirred considerable excitement throughout the state. Captain Bunch had replaced politics as the major topic of conversation. Suddenly, he was spotted simultaneously in dozens of places. In Baton Rouge, he was believed to have been seen riding a train through the city. A posse was organized and went in pursuit. The man who was identified as Bunch learned about it and, to avoid being shot on sight by a trigger-happy posse, sneaked into the State Penitentiary to get the case of mistaken identity ironed out.[4]

Jackson and Summers returned to Franklinton on Friday morning, both men firmly committed to the capture or death of the two remaining outlaws. They were joined there by three remaining members of the posse: John Jackson, Dave Martin, and Monroe McElveen. Taking Ben Duncan with them from the parish prison, the posse left that evening and rode all night through the woods and swamps to the vicinity of the Curnell's house in Marion County. It was subsequently rumored in New Orleans that Duncan had been taken from the jail by friends of Sherling and lynched, but this was later revealed as untrue.

At daybreak, Saturday, August 20, the posse arrived in the area and checked several houses where the Curnell might be hiding, including one place where two lady friends, "Sis" Terrell and Delia Hunt, lived. But there was no trace of him. The tired and hungry men went to Duncan's place where he cooked breakfast for them while the horses were fed and groomed. The posse remained at the farm resting that afternoon. Jackson and Summers, however, felt they were much too close to stop now.

Convinced that the Curnell had to be in the area and receiving assistance from his brother, the two detectives lay in some weeds near Rob Hobgood's house that afternoon and evening. Finally, after darkness fell, they watched Rob Hobgood leave his house with a package the detectives thought might be food. They silently followed him into the wooded swamps, staying as close as they dared, and watched him meet a man they assumed must be the Curnell. The amount of food that the man was given seemed meant for more than one person and Jackson and Summers deduced that the Curnell and Bunch were probably in hiding together. Jubilant at the discovery, they stealthily retreated from the scene and returned to Duncan's home to get a few hours' rest.

Very early Sunday morning, August 21, the rested posse rode over to Rob Hobgood's house, but came upon him riding in their direction. Recalling the success of the tactic on Henry Carneguay, the detectives took Hobgood from his horse, put a noose around his neck, threw the rope over a tree limb, and began to pull the rope taut. The detectives forcefully demanded to know the whereabouts of his brother and Bunch. The frightened man was finally convinced that his continued denials would only result in a stretched neck and admitted that the two were in hiding together. Further, he said, when the posse stopped him he was on his way to meet and give the Curnell some money and clothes as the two outlaws were preparing to go into hiding on Honey Island.

The detectives demanded that Hobgood lead them to the location of the meeting with his brother. The prisoner told them that he was supposed to meet the two outlaws at a deserted house in Washington Parish. He agreed to lead the posse to the spot if they promised to spare the Curnell's life. Jackson agreed to avoid killing his brother "unless he showed fight, in which event he must take his chances."[5]

Forcing their horses at a killing pace, Rob Hobgood led Jackson and his posse to the vicinity of the vacant Sheridan place on the "Muster Ground," located about seventeen miles northwest of Franklinton on Muster Ground Creek. Local militia units had used the area as a camping ground years before. Jackson warned his men to be on their guard. Although it would be good to capture Bunch alive, it was most probable that he would resist. He reminded them of the widespread story that Bunch was believed to wear chain mail or some other protection against bullets and that any gunfire should be directed at his head.

Quietly, the men rode north along the narrow road leading to the Sheridan place, tall virgin pines towering above and shading the progress of their exhausted horses. The lush green vegetation flourished in the August humidity and screened any noise. At about 9:15 A. M., the posse tied its horses in a thicket to the rear of the Sheridan house, which sat on a knoll alongside the road. Cautiously, the heavily armed men approached the silent structure, watching for any signs of movement. The house was surrounded by a low fence. Immediately to the front was an open field gently sloping downhill from the house about 400 to 500 feet to a thicket of pine, oak, cedar, and hickory trees, just beyond which coursed a branch of Muster Ground Creek and a swampy area.

After a few minutes of observation, the detectives surmised that the house was empty and moved in slowly for a closer look. It was determined that the house was indeed vacant, though Cape Jasmine and Crepe Myrtle gave evidence that it had once been a home. The detectives silently moved around to the front of the house, inside the surrounding fence. Looking toward the thicket at the lower end of the field, a man could be seen and Jackson later stated that they all immediately recognized him as Eugene Bunch. Bunch stood at the edge of the open field just a few feet from the thicket, apparently unaware of the presence of the posse.

At a motion from Jackson, the posse charged toward the outlaw, most jumping over the low fence while Jackson and Summers went through the gate. When the detectives had advanced about thirty feet beyond the fence, Bunch, holding his Winchester, spotted them coming toward him. Curnell Hobgood sat on the ground about twenty feet away from him, also holding a rifle, but, as he was screened by trees, the posse could not see him.

The surprised Bunch attempted to grasp the situation. At first he hesitated, then turned and took two or three steps toward the thicket. Suddenly, he whirled around and fired a desperate shot at the oncoming detectives that whizzed harmlessly past them. The outlaw turned away from them, levering another cartridge into his rifle, and started to run for the cover of the nearby underbrush. The five members of the posse stopped and fired a volley at him almost simultaneously. Four rifle slugs slammed into the retreating outlaw's back. A fifth round struck the back of his neck, tunneled through his brain, and emerged from the center of his forehead. Dying, Bunch staggered a step, then fell face forward to the ground, his finger spasmodically tightening on the trigger of his rifle and exploding a harmless shot into the ground. The forty-nine year odyssey of Captain Bunch had ended.

The Curnell jumped to his feet and froze as the posse approached, not able to fully comprehend what was happening. When Bunch's lifeless body collapsed to the ground, Hobgood threw his rifle away and put up his hands. "Don't shoot!" he pleaded. Keeping their rifles leveled at him, the posse cautiously approached the petrified outlaw and handcuffed him.[6]

The hot Louisiana sun beat down on the seven men as they stood looking at Bunch's body. The sounds of the nearby woods returned, frightened away only briefly by the exploding violence. Rob Hobgood was sent to find a wagon in which to haul the body. He finally located the place of George Sheridan some miles away and returned after five or six hours with an ox cart. In the meantime, the detectives examined the body.

Bunch was wearing a vest, the inside lining of which was fluted and filled with brass cartridges. It was the vest that had given rise to the rumors that he wore chain mail for protection. In addition to his Winchester, the outlaw also carried two .44-caliber Colt revolvers and wore a filled cartridge belt around his waist. His shabby clothing gave him the appearance of a tramp. Among other possessions the detectives discovered at the scene were about twenty more pounds of cartridges, dynamite fuses, a magnifying glass, screwdrivers, gun cleaning equipment, field glasses, railroad guides and timetables, a pocket compass, a hypodermic syringe, four masks, a false moustache, a wig, and about thirty dollars in cash.[7] A watch and chain on his body were later identified as loot from the April robbery of the Illinois and Central.

A frightened George Sheridan brought his cart to the scene and agreed to haul Bunch's body to Franklinton for five dollars. Jackson would have preferred to have it taken to Amite City for an inquest, but the August heat was already causing rapid decomposition. Several people who lived in the area had heard about the shooting and came to see the body. An oilcloth was placed down in the ox cart and Bunch's body was laid on it. As the cart started its slow trip, Jackson and Summers went on ahead to Franklinton with Curnell Hobgood to make preparations for an inquest into Bunch's death and his burial.

The cart arrived in Franklinton about 10 P. M. and was greeted by an excited crowd. A coroner's inquest was set up, presided over by local Justice of the Peace William A. Burris. Jackson later observed that the jury seemed afraid to touch the body and the detectives had to roll up their sleeves and take the body from the cart. Several citizens of Franklinton who had known Bunch for some time, such as John R. Wood and Doctor Varnado, identified the body on the courthouse yard as that of Eugene Bunch. The jury quickly returned a verdict of death by law officers while resisting arrest.

After the inquest, Bunch's body was placed in a simple coffin. Curious crowds gathered and many cut off pieces of his clothing for souvenirs.[8] After a period of display, he was buried in an isolated spot about 200 yards east of town on a bluff overlooking a ravine through which Jones Creek ran. Only a red clay mound, a large tree overhead, and two crude pieces of wood that someone had added served to mark the grave's location.[9]

At about 2 A. M., Monday, Jackson and Summers left for Amite City with the Curnell in a springless wagon. They arrived at about 7 A. M., the presence of Hobgood creating considerable excitement. That afternoon, with a large crowd at the station, the detectives boarded the train with their prisoner and took him to New Orleans. It was their intention to get Hobgood extradited to Mississippi for the Terrell murder and the rewards being offered for him there. Tangipahoa Parish Deputy Sheriff Elzy B. Dees, however, was also en route to New Orleans carrying a commitment order from Judge Reid directing the lawman to take custody of the Curnell and place him in the Tangipahoa Parish Prison to stand trial for train robbery.

Handcuffed and wearing a broad-brimmed black felt hat with a small round crown, Hobgood was rather surly and subdued during the train ride, occasionally spitting tobacco juice out an open window at passing telegraph poles. A New Orleans reporter had difficulty trying to get him to talk. Reluctantly, Hobgood told the reporter that he had not seen Bunch since they had separated after the robbery until about 10 A. M., Saturday, August 20, when Bunch sent for him to meet him in the woods.[10] Hobgood had already told the detectives that Bunch had admitted to him the Sherling killing. He claimed that his only part in the train robbery was, like Carneguay, to stand outside the train, not shooting or intimidating anyone.

The train arrived in New Orleans at about 7:30 P. M. Monday evening, but word of the notorious prisoner had preceded it. Crowds of the curious had congregated at every station along the way, anxious to catch sight of Hobgood, some even bold enough to try to talk to him. When Jackson and Summers escorted the Curnell from the train at New Orleans, the size of the crowd at the station forced them to seek refuge in a baggage room until a carriage could be sent. They then whisked their prisoner to the Central Police Station where, with the permission of Superintendent Gaster, he was placed in a cell while a crowd gathered outside, trying to catch a glimpse of him. A reporter interviewed him before his supper arrived and Hobgood recounted his association with Bunch.[11]

For the detectives, it was a time to light up cigars and celebrate the end of the hunt. They willingly told and retold the details of the chase, clearly enjoying the public attention. Jackson commented on the visits Bunch had reportedly made to other states, quipping, "I think he'll spend the rest of his time in Louisiana." Jackson felt that the bandit was "very much overestimated by the public," explaining that Bunch had "no more education than the ordinary Mississippi hayseed." The detective added that, while Bunch was goodhearted, jovial, and brave, his selection of and confidence in "such ignoramuses as Carneguay and Hobgood" did not speak well for his judgment.[12]

In Dallas, a reporter carried the news of her former husband's death to Flavia Bunch. Her response was, simply, that she "deplored his misspent life on account of her son," adding that drawings of the outlaw in the newspapers did not resemble him.[13] In Gainesville, Bunch's fate was the major topic of conversation. The local newspaper concluded: "A volume might be written of his crimes, but they are ended now. He ended as all men must who accept his methods."[14]

Other newspapers continued to attempt to piece together the facts of Bunch's life and death, here and there exaggerating or concocting fanciful deeds. These were romanticized seeds from which legends are often derived. In one article, Bunch was referred to as the "Prince of Outlaws,"[15] while another used the term "fearless and irrepressible gang of freebooters."[16] The story was printed that Bunch had once been a "big loser" in a land suit with a railroad company and that he had vowed to get even with the railroads.[17] He was repeatedly confused with the Rube Burrow gang and credited with many of its exploits. In building a larger-than-life image, it was claimed that he had once been arrested by the Texarkana City Marshal, only to pull a concealed pistol, disarm the lawman, and lock him in his own jail, a story very similar to that told about Dallas and Lum Johnson.[18] And, of course, as with so many other outlaws, there was the obligatory "Robin Hood" perspective, crediting Bunch with giving money to a needy family.[19] One newspaper wrote with tongue in cheek: "No wonder the great train robber was instantly killed. All the shots from the posse seem to have struck him in a bunch."[20]

On Tuesday morning, August 23, curious crowds assembled around the New Orleans police station again, believing rumors that the Curnell was going to be taken to the train station for a trip to Mississippi. Detectives Jackson and Summers came to the station and talked privately several times with Hobgood. C. C. Jarvis, the engineer of the Illinois Central train, and the fireman at the time of the robbery came to the station to view the prisoner to see if they could recognize him as one of the robbers. When Hobgood walked into Superintendent Gaster's office, Jarvis identified him positively as one of the bandits, claiming that it was Hobgood who had held two pistols on him in the cab. The fireman, however, was unable to identify the Curnell and left the station. Jarvis and the Curnell shook hands and discussed the robbery, Hobgood still insisting that he had only been acting under Bunch's directions. Hobgood and Jarvis both returned to the Curnell's cell where they continued their conversation. A large number of people were also allowed to enter the station and pass by the cell to both see and talk with Hobgood.[21]

Deputy Sheriff Dees of Tangipahoa Parish presented the commitment order from Judge Reid to Superintendent Gaster. Tom Jackson had already telegraphed Louisiana Governor Murphy Foster in an effort to get the order revoked. He much preferred to see Hobgood stand trial for the more serious offense of murder and, just as importantly, add the Mississippi rewards to those given for Bunch's capture. The governor, however, refused to intervene in the matter. Hobgood was taken to the Orleans Parish Prison to stay until his status was determined.[22]

Jackson did not give up his efforts. On August 25, he met in Jackson, Mississippi, with Governor Stone and secured a formal request of the Louisiana governor to hand over Hobgood for the murder case. The next day, he delivered the requisition to Governor Foster in Baton Rouge. Foster told him that, while he had no objection to turning over the Curnell, he was going to submit the matter to the State Attorney General since both states had charges pending.[23]

Eugene Bunch was dead and buried. Henry Carneguay

was already in the penitentiary serving his term. Edward S. Hobgood, the "Curnell," was in custody and two states were demanding he stand trial for serious crimes. The outlaw trail had ended for the "Bunch Gang" in a bloody finale in the Louisiana swamps. The era of the train robber in the United States was fast drawing to a close.

NOTES

1. *New Orleans Times-Democrat*, August 23, 1892.
2. *Times-Democrat*, August 17, 1892.
3. *Times-Democrat*, August 23, 1892; *New Orleans Daily Picayune*, August 19, 1892; Minutes Book, 46th Judicial District Court, Tangipahoa Parish, Louisiana, cause no. 1142, Book 4, p. 523, August 17, 1892.
4. *Baton Rouge Daily Advocate*, August 19, 21, 1892.
5. *New Orleans Times-Democrat*, August 23, 1892.
6. *Times-Democrat*, August 23, 1892; *New Orleans Daily Picayune*, August 23, 1892; *New Orleans Delta*, August 23, 1892 (quoted in Magee, *Eugene Bunch Story*, pp. 32-41).
7. *New Orleans Times-Democrat*, November 4, 1892.
8. *New Orleans Daily Picayune*, September 15, 1892.
9. *New Orleans Times-Democrat*, September 14, 1892.
10. *New Orleans Delta*, August 23, 1892 (quoted in Magee, *Eugene Bunch Story*, pp. 32-41).
11. *New Orleans Delta*, August 23, 1892 (quoted in Magee, *Eugene Bunch Story*, pp. 32-41); *New Orleans Times-Democrat*, August 23, 1892; *New Orleans Daily Picayune*, August 23, 1892.
12. *New Orleans Times-Democrat*, August 23, 1892.
13. *New Orleans Daily Picayune*, August 23, 1892.
14. *Gainesville* (Texas) *Daily Hesperian*, August 23, 1892.
15. *New Orleans Daily Picayune*, August 19, 1892.
16. *New Orleans Times-Democrat*, August 19, 1892.
17. *Times-Democrat*, August 23, 1892. No record of any such suit has been located.
18. *New Orleans Daily Picayune*, August 23, 1892.
19. Horan and Sann, *Pictorial History*, p. 147. Old timers in Washington Parish still repeat the legend that Bunch loaned a penniless, desperate widow woman enough money to pay her rent, then robbed the heartless landlord as he left, the money still warm in his pocket. Students of western lore will recognize this as a story often told about Jesse James and other outlaws.

140 *The Train Robbing Bunch*

20. *St. Tammany* (Louisiana) *Farmer*, September 10, 1892.
21. *New Orleans Times-Democrat*, August 24, 1892; *New Orleans Daily Picayune*, August 24, 1892.
22. *New Orleans Daily Picayune*, August 24, 1892.
23. *Daily Picayune*, August 26-27, 1892; *New Orleans Times-Democrat*, August 27, 1892.

Washington Parish officials involved in the Eugene Bunch saga: seated left to right—Judge William A. Burris, District Judge Robert R. Reid, and District Attorney Bolivar Edwards; standing left to right—Court Clerk Louis A. Bickham, Sheriff Henry S. Burkhalter, and attorney Prentiss B. Carter. (Courtesy of Mrs. Zuma F. Magee.)

9 Aftermath

The rumors began almost as soon as Bunch was under the ground. It was said that Tom Jackson's version of how the bandit died was not true. People in Franklinton whispered to each other that the Curnell had made a deal with the detectives, then they killed Bunch while he lay sleeping on the ground. Other stories had Bunch suspecting Hobgood of betraying him and planning to kill Hobgood.[1]

Justice Burris, who presided over Bunch's inquest, alleged that Hobgood shot Bunch on the instructions of Jackson and that Rob Hobgood had been the intermediary between his brother and the detective. Burris claimed that, on the day that Bunch was killed, a man named Crane claimed that the Curnell came running up and asked him to go to his brother and Jackson and tell them that Bunch was dead and he was ready to surrender. Further speculation in the community was fueled by the fact that Hobgood was not injured when the posse made its charge, even though he did not throw down his rifle until Bunch was dead. Also, the efforts of the detectives to get the Curnell extradited to Mississippi, in spite of Judge Reid's commitment order, were viewed with suspicion. Finally, many looked askance at the thought that Bunch fired one shot at the five men without hitting anyone, yet every shot fired by them struck him in the back. The fact that the official version of Sherling's murder had been provided by Detective Summers led many to conclude that perhaps officials were trying to cover up Hobgood's role in that death, too.[2]

As the rumors grew stronger, Boliver Edwards, the District Attorney for Washington Parish, began to interview people who might have some knowledge of the events of August 21. Finally, hearing enough to believe there might be some substance to the stories, Edwards secured a warrant of arrest from Judge Robert Reid on Hobgood for the murder of Eugene Bunch.

Early on the morning of Thursday, September 8, 1892, the Curnell was taken from the Orleans Parish Prison and, accompanied by his brother Rob and Washington Parish Sheriff Henry S. Burkhalter, as well as Deputy W. S. Grinsby, transported by train to Amite City. He was lodged in the jail there until a preliminary examination could be held in Franklinton. The Curnell vigorously denied that he had killed Bunch. The prosecutor had asked the Southern Express Company to return the articles that the detectives had taken from Bunch's body, but the firm only returned a voucher for fifty dollars, representing the cash and personal effects taken by Jackson. Not satisfied, Edwards sent back twenty dollars, keeping the amount that had been found on the body, and insisting that the other articles be returned.[3] Edwards had hoped that some of the physical evidence might help him successfully prove that Bunch had been shot while lying down.

Governor Foster formally refused to honor the Mississippi request for Hobgood's extradition on September 10, stating that the outlaw would first have to answer to all charges pending in Louisiana. Earlier that morning, at 3 A.M., Sheriff Burkhalter had already transferred the Curnell from Amite to Franklinton.[4] Rumors continued to persist that he had killed both Bunch and Henry Sherling. Hobgood, however, insisted on his innocence and vainly asked that both Jackson and Summers be summoned as his witnesses.

The examing trial began on Tuesday morning, September 13. Franklinton's only hotel hosted all of the interested parties, ranging from Judge Reid and Edwards to Hobgood's wife, mother, and two brothers, Rob and Bill. The rumors were so strong in this rural community that feelings were now beginning to run high against Hobgood and the detectives. There were even fears of mob violence. Sheriff Burkhalter kept the Curnell under heavy guard and elaborate precautions were taken to protect his safety.

One hour before the hearing commenced, Hobgood finally secured an attorney, Prentiss B. Carter, to represent him. The weather outside threatening rain, Judge Reid called the crowded courtroom to order at about 9:30 A. M. and read the charge of murder to the Curnell, who coolly responded, "I ain't guilty." Edwards was going to try to prove that Hobgood coldbloodedly murdered Bunch while he slept, then surrendered to Jackson's posse. In turn, Jackson was supposed to have staged the shooting of Bunch by the posse several hours later so that Hobgood's perfidy would be covered and Jackson could claim credit for the apprehension of the dangerous train robber and collect any rewards.

The first witness, fifteen-year old Charles Elliott, testified that he had known Bunch, but did not know Hobgood. On the day of Bunch's death, the boy said that he had passed by the Old Sheridan place at about 7 A. M. but saw no one. At about 9 A. M., when he and his mother had come to the old house to gather vegetables and tend to chickens, Charles said he passed through the yard gate and saw Bunch lying down on the ground on his left side near the thicket, his left arm under his head, which was resting on saddle bags. Recognizing Bunch by his red sandy beard, the boy noticed that his right eye was half open, but didn't know if he was asleep or awake. Charles saw no blood and frightened, returned to tell his mother, asking her to go back home, which was about 300 yards down the road from there. He testified that he heard shots later at about eleven o'clock, not having heard any prior to that time. At about one o'clock that afternoon, the boy returned to the old Sheridan place and observed Bunch's bloody body, which had not changed its position from when he saw it about four hours earlier. His mother, Margaret Elliott, sister of George Sheridan, confirmed her son's story and recalled that she heard one single shot, then a rapid succession of shots at about eleven o'clock.

George Sheridan, who hauled Bunch's body to Franklinton, told the quiet court that, before daybreak, he heard a single loud shot from the direction of the Sheridan place, a half mile away. At about eleven, he heard as many as eighteen to twenty-eight shots from the same direction, however, he did not go there until Rob Hobgood came for the wagon. Edwards would contend that the single shot heard by Sheridan was that of the Curnell murdering a sleeping Bunch.

Edwards called to the stand Henderson Dillon, a black man who lived about three miles north of the Sheridan place. The nervous Dillon testified that he thought that he saw the Curnell riding with five other horsemen earlier that Sunday morning and that the man wanted to borrow a pony, their conversation carried on over a 150-yard distance. He said he thought it was the same man the posse had later. Charles Sheridan and Bill Hunt both testified that they saw Bunch and the bullet wound in his forehead at about noon, Hunt declaring that the wound was fresh.

Charles Crane, Hobgood's brother-in-law, testified that Rob Hobgood had borrowed a black pony that Sunday morning. Edwards asked him if the Curnell had also visited him and asked him to notify Rob and Jackson that Bunch was dead and he was willing to surrender. Crane denied this, even though Edwards persisted that he would prove that it was true. Wilbur Tullos, 14, however, said he definitely saw the Curnell pass by the house of Charles Crane's brother, William, about sun-up and spoke to him. He recalled that the Curnell said he was going home. Another witness, Preston Thomas, said that he saw the

Curnell enter Charles Crane's house, then saw Crane leave in the direction of Rob Hobgood's place, although cross-examination by Carter caught him in several discrepancies.

Mrs. Charles Crane, Hobgood's sister, admitted that the Curnell had visited their house Saturday, not on Sunday, but contradicted her husband's testimony by declaring that Rob Hobgood had not borrowed a horse. She denied that she ever told Judge Burris or lawyer Carter that the Curnell had come to their house on Sunday, claiming that the detectives had rattled her and had even put "a pistol at my mother's breast."

In an effort to clear the point, Hobgood's attorney was sworn over his objections and put on the stand. He told the court that he had been at the Crane house after the shooting in the employ of the posse, who wanted the reward, not as the Curnell's attorney. He protested that he had learned some things that day which, in his present role, were now privileged. Pressed by Judge Reid, Carter finally admitted that Mrs. Crane told him that the Curnell had been there. Judge Burris confirmed that statement.

Rob Hobgood recalled for the court the detectives' threat to lynch him if he didn't lead them to his brother. However, when the posse had circled the Sheridan place, he had stayed behind and only heard a single shot followed by a volley. Although Jackson and Summers were not present at the hearing, Ben Duncan and Monroe McElveen testified as to the detectives' version.

The Curnell then briefly made a statement: "The thing is this. . . I know one thing. . . they killed my partner and captured me. The first I saw of them, they were all around us there. It wasn't but a flash before they were shooting. I saw I was going to be killed and threw up my hands." The Judge considered digging up Bunch's body to determine the number of bullet holes in his clothing, but, since the clothing had been so badly cut up by the crowd at the courthouse, it was doubted that there would be anything of evidentiary value. The inquest report was determined to be adequate for a description of his wounds.

On Wednesday, a statement made by the Curnell was read to the court. He testified that he and Bunch had slept on the ground outside the house and at daylight, while Bunch continued sleeping, he arose and saw the Elliott boy, who ran off. A little after sun-up, Bunch arose, he said, and the two ate. He denied passing by Henderson Dillon's place or going to see his sister. The Curnell also declared that he had never seen Tom Jackson before then.

In the afternoon, at the conclusion of testimony, Judge Reid remanded Hobgood to jail without bail until he could be tried for Bunch's murder. The conflicting testimony had raised a sufficient doubt and there were some witnesses, according to Edwards, who had not been heard from. Because the Washington Parish jail was not adequate, it was decided to transfer the Curnell that evening back to the parish prison in New Orleans.[5] Considering the very real possibility of a lynch mob at Amite City, Sheriff Burkhalter took his prisoner back to Orleans Parish very early the next morning by way of Covington.

During the next month, the Washington Parish Grand Jury began to consider the Hobgood case, but initially had difficulty getting organized because the required swearing of the court clerk had been overlooked. This presented the possibility that, if subsequently indicted, the Curnell's trial might have to be delayed until the next District Court term. However, on October 19, an indictment for Bunch's murder was returned and Hobgood's attorney asked for an immediate trial.[6] Deputy Sheriff T. D. Bennett, in an elaborate scheme, nervously whisked Hobgood from New Orleans by train the next afternoon to Covington and that evening, with other guards, went by horseback through the dark woods to Franklinton, sneaking him into the jail at 5 A. M.[7] Later that morning, Hobgood was arraigned, pleaded not guilty, and asked for a jury trial. In addition to P. B. Carter, he also secured Joe Reid, the brother of the judge, as an attorney.

It was rumored that some of the prosecutor's best witnesses were afraid to testify and had left the state. While some alleged that this was a result of fear of Hobgood's friends, others claimed that Tom Jackson was in the area and influencing witnesses to hurriedly depart.[8] On Tuesday, October 25, when Hobgood's trial was scheduled to begin, a number of key witnesses actually did not appear. After a delay of several hours to see if they might show up, Edwards asked for a continuance. Although the judge indicated that sworn testimony taken at the preliminary hearing would be acceptable for this trial, Edwards responded that there were other witnesses who were not here, who had not testified earlier, and who would be important to the prosecution. Judge Reid granted the continuance. The next day Hobgood was once more back in the safekeeping of the Orleans Parish Prison to await another trial.[9]

While Hobgood languished in jail, a number of events occurred which were related to the Bunch story. In October, the Southern Express Company had returned the dead outlaw's personal effects to Washington Parish officials, including his dapple grey stallion. On November 5, the effects were auctioned off from the courthouse steps to an interested crowd. Lee Powers, a Covington policeman, paid $350 for the horse, fifty dollars for Bunch's Winchester, and forty dollars for his two revolvers. The Curnell's horse sold for $125. Powers intended to take the articles to Chicago for exhibition.[10] But another incident at this same time introduced a bizarre irony to the story.

When Detective Charles Summers had been stationed in Meridian, Mississippi, for the Southern Express Company prior to his involvement in the hunt for Bunch's gang, a package containing over $150 was stolen from the express office there. Later, a box of silver worth $1,000 was also missed and both Summers and Tom Jackson were assigned to investigate the case. The containers were never found.

Summers and Night Clerk Kennedy were in the Meridian office of the express company on the evening of Tuesday, December 6, 1892. Kennedy placed a package containing $5,000 into the office safe, locked it, and went out in the cold night to meet an incoming train. When he returned and opened the safe later, the package was missing. Summers claimed ignorance and notified the supervising express agent of the loss. He and Jackson conducted an investigation until Saturday, December 10, when Summers boarded the train for New Orleans. However, when his train reached Hattiesburg, he was arrested by local police on the basis of a telegram from Jackson. Apparently, Jackson concluded that only one person could have taken the money. That evening, Jackson and Detective John Horne escorted Summers back to Meridian. A search of his person turned up $450 and he was placed under guard in a hotel.

Summers subsequently confessed that he had obtained a key to the safe and had taken the money. The key and the money were given to a friend from his Chicago days, Tom Murray. A week later, Murray had been nabbed and returned by detectives to Meridian from Chicago and had confessed his part in the crime. A total of $3,640 was recovered from him and he admitted that he had purchased jewelry in New Orleans, lost money at the races and at poker, and given $550 to Summers.

On January 3, 1893, indictments were returned against both men and they plead guilty without the benefit of an attorney. They were sentenced on February 2 to five years each in the Mississippi State Penitentiary.[11] Both men entered the penitentiary three days later, Summers assigned number 338 and Murray, 364. Apparently prison life did not agree with the former detective. On August 7, 1893, Summers escaped, but he was subsequently caught and returned to the penitentiary on December 29, 1893. He escaped again on April 8, 1894, and there is no record that he ever returned. Murray, on the other hand, was a model prisoner and earned sufficient "good time" to be released from prison on August 2, 1895.[12]

In the meantime, one of the former members of the Jackson posse was not happy with the share of the reward that he had received. Monroe McElveen wrote Superintendent Fisher of the Southern Express Company expressing his displeasure. The letter was turned over to Jackson and, on January 31, 1893, the detective wrote a letter from Chattanooga, Tennessee, to McElveen:

> Friend Monroe,
>
> Yours of the 5th to Mr. Fisher reached me today. I am sorry you think I have treated you wrong. I did not intend to. I have been wanting to get down to see you for three months but I have not had the time. Monroe I will say in regard to the reward that it was offered for the capture of the parties. You know that there was none captured but Carneguia. But that makes no difference. I know that you let Henry have your horses and fed him. Of course if he had not got killed and could have got the men it would have been good money to you both. Will eighty dollars satisfy you besides what you have got. That is more than any of the rest got that was on that trip. If that will satisfy you I am satisfied that Mr. Fisher will instruct me to pay it. Write me at Aberdeen and if you think this all right I will meet you at Osyka and pay you. Write in recept of this with kind regards to you and family I am your friend.
>
> T. V. Jackson[13]

Apparently, McElveen was dissatisfied with this response and did not respond. On February 28, from Aberdeen, Jackson sent him another letter, this time being a little more direct:

> Friend Monroe
>
> Why is that I don't hear from you. I wrote you sev-

eral weeks ago stating that I would advise Supt. Fisher to pay you eighty dollars more than what you had got and that would be more than any one else got. You spoke about there being four thousand dollars offered Henry. There was never but one thousand dollars offered for the capture and conviction of the three men.

Henry was offered one thousand for the capture of these men or put them where I could get them. Unfortunately for Henry he was killed before he done this job he taken the chances for the thousand and lost his life whitch I regret as much as you do. I regret your placing yourself in the position you have but I did not force you to do it. You went with me I thought to revenge the death of Henry. The Southern Express Company is willing to pay for any services rendered but they don't want to settle for everyboddy's trouble. Will Jones has put in a claim for fifty dollars which has been settled. I did not think he would want the Southern Express Company to pay him for the killing of the son of a bitch that killed his relative especially when he had nothing to do with the killing. Write me if you are willing to take the eighty dollars and I will either come to your house or you can meet me at Osyka. Write on recipt.

Your friend
T. V. Jackson[14]

There is no record as to McElveen's response.

Hobgood was escorted from the Orleans Parish Prison on Monday afternoon, March 27, 1893, by Sheriff Burkhalter and four heavily-armed guards. All but two witnesses had been accounted for and the trial for Bunch's murder was once more set. The Curnell was lodged in the Franklinton jail amid persistent rumors that Tom Jackson would like an opportunity to silence him before he had a chance to reveal some heretofore unrevealed secret about Bunch's death.[15]

The trial began on Thursday morning, March 30, Joe Reid acting as Hobgood's defense attorney. After a jury was finally selected, Edwards began the questioning of witnesses. The testimony was essentially the same as that at the preliminary hearing, although Henderson Dillon was more positive now that he had seen the Curnell ride by his place with the posse, correcting his earlier testimony. At the end of the day, a recess was declared until Saturday morning for observance of Good Friday.[16]

On the front page of Saturday's *New Orleans Times-Democrat*, a startling story alleged that a crowd of men had surprised the Washington Parish jailer and his deputies on Friday night and had freed Curnell Hobgood. According to the article, one deputy had been critically wounded in the encounter and the body of one of Hobgood's rescuers was found not far away.[17] However, the story was a hoax and, embarrassed, the newspaper made no further reference to the alleged incident.

More testimony was taken on Saturday, Wilbur Tullos and Preston Thomas again telling the court that they had seen the Curnell at Charles Crane's on the morning that Bunch was killed. Charles Crane again took the stand and admitted that, on the fateful Sunday morning, not only had Rob Hobgood borrowed a horse, the Curnell was there just after sun-up and asked him to go to Rob and tell him to bring some grub and money to the old Sheridan place. Crane said he complied with the request, although the Curnell said nothing at all about Bunch. At the completion of testimony that day, the trial was continued on Monday.

On April 3, after the prosecution completed its presentation, Hobgood's attorney, Joe Reid, felt that Edwards had not made a case against the Curnell and decided not to introduce any testimony. Both sides then presented their arguments to the jury. After deliberating for about three hours, the jury found the Curnell not guilty. "Thank you, gentlemen," responded a relieved Hobgood. He was then returned to New Orleans to await action on the train robbery charge,[18] but this time the amount of security was greatly reduced.

Because of the conflicting statements, not everyone was happy with the jury verdict. Bunch had been well thought of by some and had already begun taking on a Robin Hood aura as legend began to replace fact. The idea that a trusted comrade could get away with such a treacherous act did not set well. To this day, members of the Hobgood family are convinced that the Curnell killed Bunch, not to make a deal with the detectives, but because Bunch had threatened to kill him, reportedly telling him he could "kiss his wife goodby." In their eyes, it was an act of self-defense.[19]

The State of Mississippi still had not given up efforts to return Hobgood to its jurisdiction for the Terrell murder. In March, I. O. Magee, sheriff of Marion County, had obtained another requisition to ask Governor Foster to give up the Curnell. The governor indicated that he was willing to fulfill this request and Sheriff Magee went to New Orleans to retrieve the prisoner. However, Orleans Parish Sheriff Remy Klock heard about the transaction and beseeched the governor to keep Hobgood for trial in Amite City for train robbery. The governor agreed and changed his mind, sending Magee back to Mississippi empty-handed.[20]

Hobgood was once more removed from his New Orleans jail cell on June 6, 1893, and taken to Amite City to stand trial. Boliver Edwards, finding the original robbery indictment was legally insufficient, filed a new bill of information that same day recharging him with the crime. The trial began on Friday, June 9, with Joe Reid asking to be removed as the Curnell's attorney. Three other attorneys, Duncan, Sentell and McKenzie, were appointed to replace him. Curiously, the first witness, C. C. Jarvis, the engineer who had so positively identified Hobgood immediately after his capture, could not identify him now as one of the train robbers. There being no other eyewitness, the only other primary evidence that could be introduced was the

Curnell's confession. During the testimony, one juror was excused for illness and another was fined for talking to a witness in the case.[21] The next day, Hobgood was the sole witness for the defense, claiming that his confession was solicited by Jackson and Summers at gunpoint. He also stated that, in return for a confession, he had been promised that he would not be prosecuted and would receive half of the $1,000 reward for Bunch.

After both sides had presented their arguments, Judge Reid charged the jury as to the law prevailing in the case and the different verdicts it could reach. As a lesser alternative to the charge of robbery, if it did not acquit Hobgood, the jury could also return a finding of guilty of grand larceny or even of petty larceny. The jury deliberated briefly for about thirty minutes, then returned a verdict of guilty on a reduced charge of grand larceny, recommending mercy by the court for the defendant. Judge Reid deferred sentencing until Monday and remanded Hobgood back to jail.

On Monday, June 12, Hobgood's attorneys filed a surprise motion calling for Hobgood's complete discharge in the case. Under Louisiana law, no person could be prosecuted for robbery or lesser included offenses unless the indictment or information was filed within one year of the offense. Since the train robbery had occurred on April 14, 1892, and District Attorney Edwards had filed an amended information on June 6, 1893, the attorneys argued that the jury's verdict was nullified. Judge Reid sustained the motion and, amazingly, the remaining member of one of Louisiana's most notorious bandit teams had escaped punishment for his crime. That evening, he was returned to New Orleans to be held for Mississippi authorities. The State of Louisiana had no further claim on him and he was removed to Mississippi shortly thereafter to face murder charges.[22]

The disposition of the murder charges in Mississippi is unknown, but Hobgood did not go to the penitentiary. While he was in jail, his wife, Shug, had given birth to a daughter. Upon his release the Curnell claimed that it was not his child and he left his wife. Hobgood remarried Cordelia or Delia Hunt, who subsequently gave him ten children. Interestingly, he named one of his sons Thomas Virgil after the detective who so diligently pursued him and Bunch.[23] Hobgood moved his family away from the Marion County area to Delhi, Louisiana, where he was involved in cotton farming.

The Curnell, though known as a "good man," still liked his whiskey and family members recall that he could be mean when he had too much. After the cotton was delivered to the gin, however, he could be counted on to play the fiddle for impromptu local dances and it was not uncommon for him to stay out all night. In late October, 1921, young Tom Hobgood's mother sent him out to look for his father when he had not returned home. In front of a house in Madison Parish, he found his father's body, stabbed twice through the upper left breast. A man who called himself John Wells, accompanied by a red-haired woman, told the shocked boy that he had stood by to "keep the goats off him."

The body lay where it was until an inquest was held, then the men making up the jury took the body home. The Hobgood family washed and dressed the body, then it was placed in a simple box and sent by train to Tylertown, Mississippi. The Curnell's son from his first marriage, Joe Reed Hobgood, delivered the body of his father to the small Hobgood plot in what is now Walthall County and he was laid to rest next to his brother Rob, who died in 1915.[24] The true story as to how Eugene Bunch died went to the grave with him and the controversy continues today.

Henry Carneguay, the remaining member of the "gang", only served two years of his five-year term, according to one source. In an interview a half century later, his brother stated that the would-be bandit became involved in a domestic squabble with his sister's husband and "got his head broke." He supposedly died in 1899.[25]

Washington Parish Sheriff Henry Slidell Burkhalter oversaw stringent security measures for Curnell Hobgood and was accidently killed in 1899 while searching for outlaws. (Courtesy of Mrs. Zuma F. Magee.)

From his involvement in the first train robbery in 1888, Joseph Leon Pounds returned to the straight and narrow. As he rose to prominence in Washington Parish, his connection with Bunch was totally forgotton. Pounds served on the Parish Police Jury for many years and as its President for sixteen years. His leadership was credited for the construction of a new courthouse and jail in the late 1890's. After 1910, he served as a postmaster in Rio, Louisiana, and operated a small grocery store. He died on August 25, 1915.[26]

Of those who Captain Bunch left behind, Flavia and young T. C. moved from Gainesville to a small residence on Crutchfield Street in Dallas. To support herself, Flavia taught in a private school. Theodore was a carrier for the Dallas *Morning News*, then became a clerk in 1891 for the Meyer Brothers Drug Company. In 1896, he returned to the *Morning News* as a route agent, Living with his mother until 1897.[27] At that time, he married Johnnie Norris of Dallas and, in July of 1898, a daughter, Jimmie Louise, was born.[28]

At the turn of the century, Flavia was living with her sister, Minerva, and Minerva's husband, grocer Henry Wilkerson. T. C. and his family lived in the town of Bowie in Montague County where he was a salesman.[29] Apparently, possessing a restless spirit much like his father's, T. C. attempted a number of enterprises without a great deal of success. In 1905, he was sued by a man who wanted the goods, wares, and fixtures of a business at Handley, Texas, placed into receivership. The motion was denied and the suit was subsequently dismissed.[30] He was briefly the proprietor of the Lake Erie Cafe in Fort Worth during 1906,[31] and he and his growing family lived in that city.

In 1907, T. C. and A. A. Hammond, among others, were sued in Fort Worth by the Missouri, Kansas, and Texas Railroad and enjoined from scalping "homeseekers tickets." These were railroad tickets sold twice a month at reduced rates to induce people to move to the area.[32] Living on Lipscomb Street in

Aftermath 157

Fort Worth, T. C. became a traveling salesman for the H. W. Williams wholesale drug company.[33] On Tuesday, March 16, 1909, after an operation for appendicitis, Theodore C. Bunch died, leaving his wife, a son, and two daughters. His body was sent to Dallas where he was buried in Oakland Cemetery.[34]

After Henry Wilkerson died, Minerva and her sister lived together for the rest of their lives. Minerva's three daughters and one son grew up and left home. Flavia, though she was getting on in years, was credited with a number of charitable activities, including the rearing of seventeen orphaned children. On Sunday, June 7, 1936, the day the Texas Centennial opened at the fairgrounds in Dallas, Flavia died of apoplexy at their home on West Seventh Street in the Dallas suburb of Oak Cliff.[35] A month later, on July 11, Minerva joined her sister in death. They both were buried in Dallas' Oakland Cemetery.[36]

The world as Eugene Bunch knew it is gone. The tall virgin pines of Washington Parish have long since been cut down and smaller trees have taken their place. Cotton farming has been replaced by the more predominant dairy industry. The contemporary problems of the complex Twentieth Century have come to overshadow the simpler life of long ago, except in the minds of those who can still remember and who serve as a living bridge between the present and the past.

The remains of Eugene Bunch today rest beneath a marble marker in a small cemetery behind a large dairy about a mile east of Franklinton. During the 1930's, after his first gravesite began to erode, he was moved to his present resting place, some say by a former student or perhaps a girl friend.[37] For the most part, Eugene Bunch is forgotten. But even today in Washington Parish, as in Cooke County, oldtimers occasionally recall the local legends of the bold and desperate highwayman. And perhaps, as with many other legends, there may even be a grain of truth.

THE END

NOTES

1. *Dallas Morning News*, August 26, 1892.
2. *St. Tammany* (Louisiana) *Farmer*, September 10, 1892.
3. *Farmer*, September 10, 1892; *New Orleans Daily Picayune*, September 9, 1892.
4. *Daily Picayune*, September 11, 1892.
5. *Daily Picayune*, September 14-15, 1892; *New Orleans Times-Democrat*, September 14-15, 1892; *St. Tammany* (Louisiana) *Farmer*, September 17, 1892.
6. *New Orleans Daily Picayune*, October 14, 18, 1892; *New Orleans Times-Democrat*, October 20, 1892.
7. *Times-Democrat*, October 21, 1892.
8. *Times-Democrat*, October 22, 1892.
9. *Times-Democrat*, October 23, 26-27, 1892.
10. *Times-Democrat*, November 4, 1892; *St. Tammany* (Louisiana) *Farmer*, November 26, 1892.
11. *New Orleans Times-Democrat*, December 12-13, 18, 1892, January 4, 1893, February 3, 1893.
12. Discharge Records, Vol. 22; Sergeant's Daily Report, Vol. 25; Department Book, Vol. 33; Mississippi State Penitentiary.
13. Magee, *Eugene Bunch Story*, p. 29. The original letter is in the possession of Mrs. Gary Stafford, Franklinton, Louisiana.
14. Magee, *Eugene Bunch Story*, p. 30.
15. *New Orleans Times-Democrat*, March 28-29, 1893.
16. *Times-Democrat*, March 31, 1893.
17. *Times-Democrat*, April 1, 1893.
18. *Times-Democrat*, April 2, 4, 1893.
19. Interview with Thomas V. Hobgood, West Monroe, Louisiana, August 13, 1981.
20. *New Orleans Times-Democrat*, April 9, 22, 1893.
21. Minute Book, 46th Judicial District Court, Tangipahoa Parish, Book 4, p. 613.
22. *New Orleans Times-Democrat*, June 7, 10-11, 13, 17-18, 26, 1893.
23. Interview with Thomas V. Hobgood, West Monroe, Louisiana, August 13, 1981.
24. Interview with Thomas V. Hobgood, West Monroe, Louisiana, August 13, 1981. Thomas Hobgood, who learned most of his father's exploits from his mother, is convinced that his father shot Bunch. As to his father's death, he recalls that some years later he ran into the red-haired woman who told him that John Wells had not given his true name, but

what connection this had with the Curnell's death was not explained to him.

One version of how Hobgood died has been passed down that the Curnell got drunk at a local dance and friend put him on a wagon, directing a boy to drive him home. Hobgood, however, became abusive with the boy, who, afraid of the former train robber, defended himself by stabbing the Curnell with a shoe awl, similar to an ice pick. The body fell off the wagon and the boy fled. (Interview with Mrs. Rastus Hobgood, Walthall County, Mississippi, August 8, 1981.)

A son-in-law of the Curnell remembered him as a "good man" who never admitted killing Bunch, but who "nodded" when the old stories were discussed. (Interview with Jim Erwin, Bogalusa, Louisiana, August 8, 1981.)

The Curnell's grave at one time had a marker, but it has been removed for many years.

25. "Louisiana's Great Train Robber," *New Orleans Times-Picayune, Dixie* Magazine, June 4, 1950.

26. *Bogalusa* (Louisiana) *Daily News*, August 13, 1953.

27. Dallas City Directory, 1893-1898.

28. *Dallas Daily Times Herald*, October 10, 1898.

29. Twelfth U. S. Census, 1900, Dallas County, Texas; Montague County, Texas.

30. Minutes, 17th District Court, Tarrant County, Texas, cause no. 24276, Vol. A5, pp. 191, 586; September 29, 1905.

31. *Fort Worth Record*, June 19, 1906.

32. Minutes, 48th District Court, Tarrant County, Texas, cause no. 26468, Vol. 20, pp. 365, 376; *Fort Worth Record*, November 12, 1907, December 22, 1907.

33. Fort Worth City Directory, 1907-1908.

34. *Fort Worth Record*, March 17, 1909; Bureau of Vital Statistics, Texas Department of Health, Certificate of Death no. 55628, March 16, 1909. His eldest daughter, Jimmie Louise, married Mathew Hennes and, as of 1937, was living in Hollywood, California. His oldest daughter, who became Mrs. Theo Dell Buehrig, and his son Norris, have not been located.

35. *Dallas Morning News*, June 8, 1936; Bureau of Vital Statistics, Texas Department of Health, Certificate of Death no. 29827, June 7, 1936.

36. *Dallas Morning News*, July 12, 1936; Bureau of Vital Statistics, Texas Department of Health, Certificate of Death no. 35029, July 11, 1936.

37. Daunton Gibbs, "Eugene Bunch" in Magee, *Eugene Bunch Story*, p. 10.

Bibliography

BOOKS

Agee, George W. *Rube Burrow, King of Outlaws.* Chicago: M. A. Donohue & Company, 1890.

Bartholomew, Ed. *Biographical Album of Western Gunfighters.* Houston: The Frontier Press of Texas, 1958.

Bartlett, Napier. *Military Record of Louisiana.* Reprint edition. Baton Rouge: Louisiana State University Press, 1964.

Biographical and Historical Memoirs of Louisiana. Vol. 1. Chicago: The Goodspeed Publishing Company, 1892.

Biographical Souvenir of the State of Texas. Chicago: F. A. Battey & Company, 1889.

Booth, Andrew B. *Records of Louisiana Confederate Soldiers and Commands.* Vol. II. New Orleans: Louisiana Military Records Commission, 1920.

Breihan, Carl W. *Outlaws of the Old West.* New York: Signet Books, 1980.

Catton, Bruce. *Never Call Retreat.* New York: Doubleday & Company, Inc., 1965.

Catton, Bruce. *Grant Takes Command.* Boston: Little, Brown & Company, 1968.

Confederate Military Service. Vol. X. Atlanta: Confederate Publishing Company, 1899.

Cox, William R. *Luke Short and His Era.* Garden City, New

York: Doubleday & Company, Inc., 1961.
Cunningham, Edward. *The Port Hudson Campaign.* Baton Rouge: Louisiana State University Press, 1963.
Dillon, Richard. *Wells, Fargo Detective.* New York: Coward-McCann, Inc., 1969.
Dorsey, Sarah A. *Recollections of Henry Watkins Allen.* New York: M. Doolady, 1866.
Harvey, Paul Jr. *Old Tige: General William L. Cabell, CSA.* Hillsboro, Texas: Hill Junior College, 1970.
Hoole, William Stanley. *The Saga of Rube Burrow.* University, Alabama: Confederate Publishing Company, 1981.
Horan, James D. *The Pinkertons.* New York: Bonanza Books, 1967.
Horan, James D. and Paul Sann. *Pictorial History of the Wild West.* New York: Bonanza Books, 1954.
Johnson, Frank W. *A History of Texas and Texans.* Vol. III. Chicago: The American Historical Society, 1914.
Jones, C. N. *Early Days in Cooke County.* Gainesville, Texas: C. N. Jones, 1936.
Magee, Zuma F. (ed.). *The Eugene F. Bunch Story.* Franklinton, Louisiana: Zuma F. Magee, 1975 (unpublished manuscript).
Mallon, Lucille Simms. *Noxubee County, Mississippi, Marriages, 1834-1869.* Noxubee County, Mississippi: Lucille Simms Mallon, 1975.
Men of Texas: A Collection of Portraits. Houston, Texas: The Houston Post, 1903.
Menn, Joseph Karl. *The Large Slaveholders of Louisiana, 1860.* New Orleans: Pelican Publishing Company, 1964.
Morgan, Jonnie R. *The History of Wichita Falls.* Wichita Falls, Texas: Nortex Offset Publications, Inc., 1971.
Nash, Jay Robert. *Bloodletters and Badmen.* New York: M. Evans & Company, Inc., 1973.
Paddock, Capt. B. B. *A Twentieth Century History and Biographical Record of North and West Texas.* Vol. I. Chica-

go: The Lewis Publishing Company, 1906.
(Patrick, Robert). *Reluctant Rebel*, ed. F. Jay Taylor. Baton Rouge: Louisiana State University Press, 1959.
Pinkerton, William A. *Train Robberies and Train Robbers*. Reprint edition. Fort Davis, Texas: Frontier Book Company, 1968.
Ray, Bright. *Legends of the Red River Valley*. San Antonio: The Naylor Company, 1941.
Smith, A. Morton. *The First 100 Years in Cooke County*. San Antonio: The Naylor Company, 1955.
Stanley, F. *Longhair Jim Courtright*. Denver: World Press, Inc., 1957.
Winters, John D. *The Civil War in Louisiana*. Baton Rouge: Louisiana State University Press, 1963.

ARTICLES

Carter, Prentiss. "The History of Washington Parish, Louisiana, as compiled from the Records and Traditions," *Louisiana Historical Quarterly*, Vol. 13, No. 1 (January 1931), p. 52.
Gibbs, Daunton. "Eugene Bunch," *The Eugene Bunch Story*, ed. Zuma F. Magee, 1975, p. 10 (unpublished manuscript).
Kendall, John Smith. "Recollections of a Confederate Soldier," *Louisiana Historical Quarterly*, Vol. 29, No. 4 (October 1946), pp. 1048-49.
Kendall, John Smith. "Muster Rolls of the Fourth Louisiana Regiment of Volunteers, CSA," *Louisiana Historical Quarterly*, Vol. 30, No. 2 (April 1947), p. 504.
"Louisiana's Great Train Robber," *Dixie* Magazine, *New Orleans Times-Picayune*, June 4, 1950.
Richards, E. Q. "Deeds of Gift or 'Love and Affection,' 1834-1869," *Mississippi Genealogical Exchange*, Vol. 25 (Spring 1979), p. 26.

NEWSPAPERS

Baton Rouge Daily Advocate, August 1892.
Birmingham (Alabama) *Age Herald*, March 4, 1889.
Bogalusa (Louisiana) *Daily News*, August 13, 1953.
Dallas Daily Times Herald, 1880, 1887-1888, 1892, 1898.
Dallas Morning News, 1886-1889, 1892, 1936.
Fort Worth Daily Gazette, 1887-1888, 1892.
Fort Worth Record, 1906-1907, 1909.
Gainesville (Texas) *Daily Hesperian*, 1888, 1892.
New Orleans Daily Picayune, 1888, 1892.
New Orleans Delta, August 23, 1892.
New Orleans Times-Democrat, 1888, 1892-1893.
San Angelo (Texas) *Standard*, 1887-1889.
St. Tammany (Louisiana) *Farmer*, 1888, 1892.
Tangipahoa (Louisiana) *Democrat*, 1874.

OFFICIAL DOCUMENTS

Cooke County, Texas:
    Marriage Certificate Book, 1882.
    Deed Records, Vols. 11-15, 17, 19-21, 23-25, 28, 38-39, 43.
    Tax Records, 1875-1885.
    Minutes, County and Commissioners Court, Vols. 1-3.
    Gainesville City Directory, 1887-1888.
    District Court Records:
        E. F. Bunch v. Francis Mathews et al, cause no. 1233, July 12, 1880.
        Waples, Painter & Co. v. E. F. Bunch, cause no. 1370, July 17, 1882.
        R. B. Sigler v. E. F. Bunch, cause no. 1411, January 15, 1883.
        A. M. Flynn v. E. F. Bunch et al, cause no. 3036, March 5, 1887.

Dallas County, Texas:
    Deed Records, Vol. 90.
    Dallas City Directory, 1884-1900.
    44th District Court Records:
        Flavia H. Bunch v. E. F. Bunch, cause no 7431, May 30, 1889.

Denton County, Texas:
    Deed Records, Vols. J, Z.

Mississippi Department of Archives and History:
    State Penitentiary Records.

Noxubee County, Mississippi:
    Deed Records, Vols. E, G, J, K.
    Record of Wills, Vol. A.

Smith County, Texas:
    General Index to Marriages, Vol. H.

St. Helena Parish, Louisiana:
    Property Transfer Book, Vol. R, p. 474.

Tangipahoa Parish, Louisiana:
    Conveyance Book, Vols. 2, 5.
    Marriage Record, Vol. 1.
    Succession Book, Vol. 1.
    6th Judicial District Court Records:
        Martha R. McDonald v. James Bunch, cause no. 38, January 25, 1870.
        Benjamin F. George v. Mrs. M. B. Bunch, cause no. 52, July 25, 1870.
    46th Judicial District Court Records:
        State of Louisiana v. Henry Carneguay, cause no. 1142, August 7, 1892.
        State of Louisiana v. E. S. Hobgood alias Colonel Hobgood, cause no. 1157, June 6, 1893.

Tarrant County, Texas:
    Deed Records, Vols. K, U, Z, 47, 51, 123.
    Fort Worth City Directory, 1907-1908.
    17th District Court Records:

John C. Harrison v. E. F. Bunch et al, cause no. 4652, November 21, 1888.

W. M. Austin v. T. C. Bunch, cause no. 24276, September 29, 1905.

48th District Court Records:
Missouri, Kansas & Texas Ry. Co. et al v. T. C. Bunch et al, cause no. 26468, November 11, 1907.

Texas State Archives:
"Widow's Application for a Pension," Book 7, No. 50758 (Flavia H. Bunch), May 16, 1932.

Texas Department of Health, Bureau of Vital Statistics:
Certificate of Death, T. C. Bunch, no. 55628, Tarrant County, Texas, March 16, 1909.

Certificate of Death, Mrs. Flavia H. Bunch, no. 29827, Dallas County Texas, June 7, 1936.

Certificate of Death, Amanda M. Wilkerson, no. 35029, Dallas County, Texas, July 11, 1936.

United States Census Records:
1850, Noxubee County, Mississippi; Smith County, Texas.
1860, East Feliciana and Washington Parishes, Louisiana.
1870, East Feliciana, Tangipahoa, and Washington Parishes, Louisiana; Smith County, Texas.
1880, Cooke County, Texas.
1900, Dallas and Montague Counties, Texas.

United States National Archives and Records Service:
"Index to Compiled Service Records of Confederate Soldiers Who Served in Organizations from the State of Louisiana."

Report of Arrest, *U. S. v. J. Leon Pounds*, Inspector M. A. Fisher, U. S. Post Office Department, November 30, 1888.

Wichita County, Texas:
Deed Records, Vols. H, I.
Minutes, Commissioners Court, Vol. 1.

LETTERS

Green, Ms. Jo, to the author, Tyler Public Library, Texas, August 14, 1981.
Horan, James D., to the author, Little Falls, New Jersey, January 10, 1981.
Magee, Mrs. Zuma F., to the author, Franklinton, Louisiana, January 15, 1981; February 5, 1981.
Richards, E. Q., to the author, Macon, Mississippi, December 8, 1980.

INTERVIEWS

Jim Erwin (son-in-law of Curnell Hobgood), Bogalusa, Louisiana, August 8, 1981.
Mrs. Rastus Hobgood, Walthall County, Mississippi, August 8, 1981.
Mr. and Mrs. Thomas V. Hobgood (son of Curnell Hobgood), West Monroe, Louisiana, August 13, 1981.
Mrs. Audrey Johnson, Walthall County, Mississippi, August 8, 1981.

The final resting place for Eugene Bunch, the Morris Cemetery, Franklinton, Louisiana. (Author's Collection.)

Index

Aberdeen, Mississippi, 115, 121, 125, 149
Addington, A. J., 56
Alexandria, Louisiana, 38
Allen, Col. Henry Watkins, 16, 17, 20, 22, n. 25
Amite City, Louisiana, 37, 38, 40, 44, 89, 93, 106-108, 110, 122, 124, 125, 130, 135, 142, 146, 152
Arcola, Louisiana, 107
Arkansas (gunboat), 21-23
Arnold, H. D., n. 72
Arnold, James C., 65, 76-77, photograph 79, 80, n. 95
Atchafalaya Bay, Louisiana, 17
Atkinson, Sophus, 77
Audubon Athletic Club, 115

Babbington Brothers, 106
Baker, John, 87
Ballinger, Texas, 92, n. 96-98
Banks, Gen. Nathanial P., 27-28, 30-33
Barrett, D. E., 47
Barrow, Col. Robert I., 16-17
Bass, Sam, photograph 45, 46, 66, n. 95
Baton Rouge, Louisiana, 21-23, 101, 130, 138
Baxter, Pete, 125, 130
Bay St. Louis, Mississippi, 16, 80
Bayou Chene, Louisiana, 17
Beauregard, Gen., 18
Beaver Creek Rifles, 14
Bellvue, Texas, 60, 66
Benbrook, Texas, 65, 68
Bennett, Dep. T. O., 146
Berwick, Louisiana, 17
Bickham, Louis A., photograph 140
Biloxi, Mississippi, 16, 44
Birmingham, Alabama, 100
Bobo, W. W., 47, 51
Bogalusa, Louisiana, 75
Bossen, D. C., 47
Bowie, Texas, 156
Boylan, Col. Thomas, 85, 86, 88, 89, n. 95-96
Bragg, Gen. Braxton, 18, 20, 21
Brashear City, Louisiana, 17
Breckinridge, Gen. John C., 21-23
Brewster, Col. O., 69
Brock, Will, 66
Bromley, Henderson, 66
Broome, O., n. 97
Brown, M. H., 60
Bryan, Beauregard, 58
Beuhrig, Mrs. Theo Dell, n. 159
Buell, Maj. Gen. Don Carlos, 18, 20
Bunch, Catherine, 12
Bunch, Cora, 44

Bunch, Eugene Franklin, birth 12, attended school 13, enlistment 14, battle of Shiloh 18-20, Port Hudson campaign 26-35, teacher 37, marriage 40, move to Texas 41, birth of son 42, political campaigns 42, 46, 48, 56, law suits against 50-51, 55-56, editor 58-59, gambling 61-64, forgeries 68-69, in New Orleans 77-81, Northeastern robbery 81-84, description 89, divorce 102-103, meets Hobgood 104, Illinois Central robbery 106-110, death 133-135, photographs 39, 117
Bunch, Flavia, 34, 40-42, 47, 50, 51, n. 52, 56, 59, 60, 64, n. 71, 102-104, 137, 156-157
Bunch, Ida Elisabeth, 44, 47, n. 53
Bunch, James (father), 12-13, 23, 37, 38, 40-41, 42
Bunch, James (brother), 42, 44, 47, 50, 56, 60
Bunch, Jimmie Louise, 156, n. 159
Bunch, Johnnie, 156
Bunch, Laura, 12, 44
Bunch, Luella, 44, 47, n. 53
Bunch, Martha (mother), 12, 38, 40-41, 42, 44
Bunch, Martha Eva (sister), 44, n. 53
Bunch, Mary Cornelia, 12, 44
Bunch, Norris, n. 159
Bunch, Theodore Conklin, 42, 47, 59-60, 102, 156-157
Bunch, Theodosius C., 12, 14, 16, 20, 33, 34, 38
Bunch, Virginia, 12-13
Burkhalter, Sheriff Henry S., photograph 140, 142, 143, 146, 150, photograph 155
Burris, Justice William A., 135, photograph 140, 141, 145
Burrow, Jim 66
Burrow, Rube, 66, 68, 92, 94, n. 99, illus. 103, 110, 115, 137

Cabell, Ben E., 65, 76, photograph 79
Caldwell, J. B., 128
Calloway, W. P., 69, n. 74
Camp Moore, Louisiana, 14, 16, 21
Camp Walker, Louisiana, 13-14
Campbell, Clay, 128
Carlock, R. L., 65
Carneguay, Henry, 105-110, 114, 128-130, 132, 136, 137-139, 154
Carr, Dave, 120

Carter, Prentiss B., photograph 140, 143, 145-147
Cason, Ben, 85
Chattanooga, Tennessee, 149
Chicago, Illinois, 115, 147, 148
Cincinnati, Ohio, 81
Clay County, Texas, 60
Cleaves, F. B., 48
Clinton, Louisiana, 40
Cloud, Isaac, 56, 60
Colorado City, Texas, 98
Comite River, 21, 23
Concho, Texas, 97
Cooke County, Texas, 11, 41-43, 46, 47, 55, 56, 64, 157
Corinth, Mississippi, 17-18, 20, 21
Costen, M. C., 65
Courtright, Longhair Jim, 62
Covington, Louisiana, 75, 80, 81, 86, 146, 147
Crane, Charles, 141, 144-145, 151
Crane, Edward, 12
Crane, Mrs. Charles, 145, 146
Crane, William, 144
Culp, J. M., 48

Dallas Morning News, 101-102, 156
Dallas, Texas, 43, 46, 55, 58, 61, 68-70, 75, 89, 92, 95, 137, 156-157
Danforth, Tommy, 115
Davis, Jefferson, 13, illus. 15, 44
Day, J. N., 48
Dees, Elzy B., 135-136, 138
DeHaven, R. C., 64
Delhi, Louisiana, 154
Denton, Texas, 44, 47, 56, 65, 69
Derby Station, Mississippi, 81
Dexter, Texas, 41, 42, 44, 50, n. 52, 55
Dillon, Henderson, 144, 146, 151
Dixon, W. H., 13
Dobkins, John W., 59
Dodge City, Kansas, 62
Donaldsonville, Louisiana, 101
Duck Hill, Mississippi, 94
Duncan, Ben J., 104-106, 116, 118, 122, 124-125, 128-131, 145
Duncan, Bob, 122-125
Duncan, Lawyer, 152
Dunn, Superintendent, 110

Earp, Wyatt, 62
East Feliciana Parish, Louisiana, 40
East Louisiana Railroad, 86
Edwards, Bolivar, 130, photograph 140, 142-144, 146, 147, 151, 152
Edwards Station, Mississippi, 21
El Paso, Texas, 64, 101
Elliott, Charles, 143, 146
Elliott, Margaret, 144

Ellis, Cora N., 69-70, n. 74, 75, 77, 85-93, n. 99
Ellis, Ira, 69-70, n. 74
Ellis, Mary, 69
Ellis, William, n. 97-98

Farragut, Admiral David, 27, 28
Farrell & Boylan's Detective Bureau, 84, 86, 88
Farrell, Michael J., n. 95-96
Faulke, Susan, 40
Fisher, H. C., 110, n. 126, 149-150
Fisher, M. A., 85, 87
Fletcher, W. L., 48
Flomaton, Alabama, n. 99
Flynn, Amanda, 40, n. 53
Flynn, Flavia (see Flavia Bunch)
Flynn, Isaac T. "Ike", 40
Flynn, Minerva (see Minerva Wilkerson)
Fort Chene, Louisiana, 17
Fort Donelson, Tennessee, 17
Fort Sumter, South Carolina, 13
Fort Worth Daily Gazette, 65, 69
Fort Worth, Texas, 44, 55, 59-62, 64-66, 68-70, 76, 89, 92, 156-157
Fort Worth & Denver Railroad, 58, 60
Foster, Gov. Murphy, 138, 142, 152
Fourth Louisiana Regiment, 14, 16-23, 28, 31
Franklinton, Louisiana, 13, 38, 106, n. 126, 128, 130-132, 134-135, 141-144, 146, 150, 157

Gainesville, Texas, 11, 42-44, 46, 48-50, 56, 58-61, 64, 65, 68, 69, 76, 89, 92, n. 94, 101, 102, 137, 156
Galveston, Texas, n. 99
Gaster, Detective, 77, 80, 85, 110, 136, 138
Gardner, Gen. Franklin, 26, 28, 30-33
Gatewood, Henry, 51
Genoa, Arkansas, 66
"Gerald, J. H.", 75, 77, 80, 81, 85, 86
Glen Lea Saloon, 68
Gordon, Texas, 60
Graham, C. G., 48
Grant, Ulysses S., 17-20, 26, 28, illus. 29, 30, 33, 34, n. 96
Gray, Long John, n. 98-99
Greenwell Springs, Louisiana, 21-22
Greensburg, Louisiana, 106
"Grice, Captain", 105, 106, 116, 118, 119
Grierson, Col. Benjamin, 28
Grinsby, W. S., 142

Hall, County Judge T. J., 48
Hammond, A. A., 156
Hammond, Louisiana, 107, 108
Handley, Texas, 156
Harger, Joel P., 69, n. 74
Harrison, JOhn C., n. 74
Harriston, Mississippi, 106, 118
Hattiesburg, Mississippi, 81, 148
Hayes, James W., 46, 48
Hebert, Detective, 87
Henderson, Captain, 92
Hennes, Mrs. Mathew (see Jimmie Louise Bunch)
Hennessy, Supt. David C., 77, 92, 93, 94, n. 113
Higgins, J. W., 110
"Hines, John ", 101
Hobgood, Bill, 143
Hobgood, Edward Scanlon ("Curnell"), 104-110, photograph 111, 114, 116, 118-125, n. 126, 128, 131-136, 139, 141-147, 150-154
Hobgood, Ida, 104, 143, 153-154
Hobgood, Joe Reed, 154
Hobgood, Robert, 104, 105, 114, 129, 131-134, 141-145, 151, 154, n. 158-159
Hobgood, Thomas Virgil, 154, n. 158
Hogan, Mrs. Charles, 77
Holliday, Doc, 62
Honey Island, 87, 93, 100, 101, 132
Honeycutt, City Marshal, 89
Horne, Detective John, 148
Houston, Texas, 61
Howeth, W. W., 65, 69, 76, photograph 91, n. 94
Hunt, Bill, 144
Hunt, Cordelia, 131, 154, 158

Illinois Central Railroad, 107, 115, 123, n. 126, 138
Independence, Louisiana, 108
Indian Territory, 56, 80, 88
Ivey, Bird, 13
Izard, Smith, n. 95

Jacks, Al, n. 98
Jackson, Harry, 50
Jackson, John, 125, 131
Jackson, Mississippi, 17, 28, 30, 110, 121, 125, 130, 138
Jackson, Thomas V., 110, 114-121, 125, n. 126, illus. 127, 128-138, 141, 142, 145-150, 153
Jarvis, C. C., 107-110, 138, 152
Jefferson County, Mississippi, 116
Johnson, Deputy Lum, 68, 137
Johnston, Gen. Albert Sidney, 17-18
Jones, W. J., 128
Jones, Will, 106, 116, 118, n. 127, 150

Kane, Jack, 125, 130
Kansas City,Missouri, 61
Kennedy, Night Clerk, 148
Kirtley, B. C., 48
Klock, Sheriff Remy, 152

Lake Erie Cafe, 156
Lamar, Justice L. Q. C., n. 99
Lamar County, Alabama, 115
Lampton, Lucious, 122
Laning, J. C., 69
Lee, Gen. Robert E., 34
Lewis, Sheriff Henry, 60
Lilly, James Bunch, 44, 47
Lilly, James F., 43-44, 47, 48, n. 53, 60
Lilly, Martha (Mattie) Caroline, 44, 47
Lincoln, Abraham, 13
Linden, Alabama, n. 99
Lindsay House, 101
Lingland, 119
Littlehale, Cora (see Cora Ellis)
Littlehale, Fred H., 69-70
Louisiana Partisan Rangers, 21-22, 30
Louisville & Nashville Railroad, n. 99
Lowrey, Charles W., 81-85

Macon, Mississippi, 12
Maddox, R. E., 64
Madison Parish, Louisiana, 154
Magee, Huey, 120-121
Magee, Sheriff I. O., 152
Magee, Warren, 128
Manassas, Battle of, 43
Marion County, Mississippi, 104, 105, 118, 122, 131, 152, 154
Martin, Dave, 125 131
Masterson, Bat, 62
Matheny, A. D., 58
Mathews, George, 108-109
McClain, Charles M., 46
McClure's Switch, 84
McComb City, Mississippi, 110
McDonald, Hugh, 12
McDonald, Martha R. (see Martha Bunch)
Mc Elroy, Henry C., 81-85
McElveen, Monroe, 121, 122, 125 131, 145, 149-150
McLendon, 80
McLennan County, Texas, n. 99
McKenzie, Lawyer, 152
McMurray, Capt. Sam, photograph 57, 76
McSpadden, G. W., 56
Meador, Elijah, 42
Meador, Elizabeth, 42
Meridian, Mississippi, 115, 147-148
Metairie Racetrace, 13
Mexico City, MExico, 101
Meyer Bros. Drug Co., 156

Miles, Col. W. R., 30
Mississippi City, Mississippi, 16
Mississippi River, 21, 26-27
Mississippi State Penitentiary, 110 148-149
Missouri, Kansas & Texas Railroad, 156
Mix, Sheriff, 110
Monroe County, Mississippi, 115
Montague County, Texas, 156
Monterey, Mexico, 101
Monterey, Tennessee, 18, 20
Moore, Governor, 14
Moorman, U. S. Marshal, 87
Morris, E. F., 46, 48, 56
Murphey, Detective, 87
Murray, Tom, 148-149
Muster Ground, 132

Nashville, Tennessee, 18
New Orleans Daily Picayune, 85, 110
New Orleans, Louisiana, 13-14, 17, 21, 23, 27, 37, 43, 44, 58, 62, 75, 77, 81, 84, 85, 89, 93, 94, n. 95-96, 107, 110, 115, 116, 121, 125, 130, 135-137, 148, 151
New Orleans & Northeastern Railway, 81, 85, 89, 93, 100
New Orleans Times-Democrat, 151
Newsome, Jim, n. 97-99
Newsom's Mill, 107, 110
Ninth Louisiana Battalion, 21, 30
Norris, Johnnie (see Johnnie Bunch)
Noxubee County, Mississippi, 12

O'Brien, Detective M. J., 110
Orleans Parish Prison, 88, 92, n. 113, 138, 142, 146, 147, 150
Osyka, Mississippi, 125, 128
Ozment, Sheriff M. M., 48

Pacific Express Co., 60, 65
Paint Rock, Texas, 97
Pearlington, Louisiana, 75, 80, 87
Pecora, Detective, 77, 80, 85
Perry, Horace, 125, 130
Phipps, M. V., 50, 51, 55-56
Pike County, Mississippi, 104, 125
Pinkerton, William, 58, n. 126
Pinkerton's Detective Agency, 58, n. 71, n. 74, 94, 115
Pipes, Amanda (see Amanda Flynn)
Pipes, John H., n. 53
Pipes, Mary H., n. 53
Pleasant Valley, Louisiana, 38
Port Hudson, Louisiana, 23, 26-34, 38
Pound, Bayles O. C., 42, 46, 47-48

Pounds, Joseph Leon, 38, n. 52, 69, 75, 80, 86-93, 94, 156
Powers, Lee, 147

Quaymas, Mexico, 101
Queen, Katie, 43

Red River National Bank, 101
Reid, Joseph, 89, 92, 122, n. 127, 147, 151, 152
Reid, Judge Robert R., 130, 136, 138, photograph 140, 141-143, 145-147, 153
Rhone, B. C., 50
Richmond, Cirginia, 58
Riggs House, 90
Rio, Louisiana, 156
Robinson, W. S., 108-109
Rollins, R. S., 46
Round Rock, Texas, 46
Ruggles, Gen. Daniel, 22, 26
Rumrill, C. C., 56
Runnels County, Texas, 92, n. 98

Sacra, J. W., 56
Salmin, M. G., 48
San Angelo, Texas, 92, n. 96-98
San Carlos, Arizona, 101
Sentell, Lawyer, 152
Sheridan, Charles, 144
Sheridan, George, 134-135, 144
Sherling, Henry, 106, 116-124, n. 126-127, 136, 141, 142, 149-150
Sherling, Ida Magee, photograph 123, n. 126
Sherman, Texas, 44
Shiloh Church, Tennessee, 18-20
Ship Island, Mississippi, 16-17
Short, Luke, 61, 62, photograph 63
Sigler, Margaret M., 44, 47, 50, n. 54, 55
Sigler, R. B., 44, 47, n. 54, 55
Skinner, W. H., 64
Smith, Henry, 88
Soule, George A., 69
Southern Express Company, 93-95, 106, 108, 110, 112, 114, 115, n. 126, 142, 147-150
Sprecht, Herman, 59
Spring, Mrs. Mary C., (see Mary Bunch)
St. Louis, Missouri, 61
St. Tammany Parish, Louisiana, 80, 101
Stone, Governor, 138
Summers, Charles O., 115, 124-125, n. 126-127, 128-138, 141 142, 145, 147-148, 153
Summit, Mississippi, 121

Tangipahoa, Louisiana, 110, 119
Tangipahoa Parish, Louisiana, 14, 37, 40, 80, 93, 101, 107, 116, 135, 138
Tarrant County, Texas, 44, 47
Taylor, Margaret S., 42
Temple, 104
Terrell, Ike, 104, 120, 135, 152
Terrell, "Sis", 131
Texarkana, Texas, 137
Texas & Pacific Railroad, 60, 64
Texas Rangers, 46, 66, 76
Third Louisiana Regiment, 14
Thirteenth Louisiana Regiment, 20
Thomas, Preston, 144-145, 151
Thompson, Alex J., 42, 46, 51, n. 52, 56
Thompson, Ben, n. 95
Thornton, Nep, 66
Tombstone, Arizona, 101
Toney, Detective, 87
Tracy, Brig. Gen. E. L., 14
Tullow, Wilbur, 144, 151
Turner, Green, 81
Tyler, Texas, 70, 74, 93
Tylertown, Mississippi, 122, 154

United States Express Company, 81, 84, 85, 89, n. 96, 101
Valentine, H. E., 47

Valentine, H. E., 47
Van Hook, 87-88
Varnado, Doctor, 135
Vera Cruz, Mexico, 101
Vernon, Indian Territory, 80
Vicksburg, Mississippi, 21, 26, 27, 28, 30, 33, 83

Waco, Texas, n. 97-99
Walker, J. R., 48
Walthall County, Mississippi, n. 113, 154
Wantland, William, 50
Waple, Painter & Co., 50
Warren, J. D., 38
Warren, W. C., 38
Washington Artillery, 43
Washington, J. R., 42
Washington Parish, Louisiana, 13, 37, 38, 40, n. 51, 80, 101, 104, 106, 116, 121, 130, 132, 142, 146, 147, 151, 156, 157
Weaver, J. H., 43
Webb, Sheriff, 110
Wells, John, 154, n. 158
Western Newspaper Union, 70
White Elephant Saloon, 62
Whiteman, Bertha, 60
Whiteman, Charles P., 60
Wichita Falls, Texas, 56-59, 69, 70, 102
Wichita Herald, 58

Wilkerson, Henry C., 60, 64, 156-157
Wilkerson, Minerva, 56, 59, 60, 64, 102, 156-157
Williams Drug Co., 157
Wingfield, Capt. James H., 14, 16, 17, 21, 28, 30, n. 36, n. 52
Wise County, Texas, 50, 56
Wood, W. Y., 128
Wright, Mrs. F. A., 47
Wright, U. S. Commissioner William, 87, 89, 93

Yates, A. S., 69, 73, n. 74

174 *The Train Robbing Bunch*

Rick Miller

Given his background in law enforcement, it's little wonder that Rick Miller has an interest in the outlaws and lawmen of the Old West. Born Richard Joseph Miller in San Diego, California, on January 20, 1941, he was raised and educated in Dallas, Texas. After a peacetime stint as an Army paratrooper, Rick joined the Dallas Police Department in 1963, rising to the rank of Lieutenant by the time he left the Department in 1975. He served as a Program Coordinator for the Texas Organized Crime Prevention Council, after which he was Chief of Police in the cities of Killeen and Denton, Texas.

Rick received his B.A. in 1970 from the University of Texas at Arlington and a Master's Degree in Public Administration from Southern Methodist University in 1974. Currently he is in his final year of studies at the Baylor University School of Law in Waco, Texas. In addition to his daughter, Shelli, Rick and his wife, Paula, are raising two boys, Lance and Stephen.

While having had a number of interests, including skydiving, cartooning, and jogging, he confesses that his "true passion" is research into the Old West and he is working on a new book about Jack Duncan, the Texas detective who played a key role in tracking down John Wesley Hardin.

F 396
.B9
U54
1983